Ultimate STYLE

From Drab to *Fab!*

Rayne Parvis Nicole Drake

Second Edition

10 9 8 7 6 5 4 3 2

Ultimate Guide to Style: From Drab to Fab / by Rayne Parvis and Nicole Drake

ISBN: 9780985804107

Library of Congress Control Number: 2012914064

StyleByRayne.com

NicoleDrake.com

Book cover design by: Jesslene Kubota of Tamayo + Kubota Design

Warning—Disclaimer

www.StyleByRayne.com

Mirror, Mirror on the wall this book is dedicated to you all!

About the Authors

Rayne Parvis and Nicole Drake

Rayne and Nicole realized that they both shared a passion for not only fashion, but also for empowering self-confidence in others. These creative and eye-for-fashion ladies spend many life changing hours providing services to people, whom they like to call **"fabulous, but…fashionably challenged."**

Rayne has always had an eclectic sense of style and before she learned the tricks of the *fashion* trade, she was, as Paris Hilton would say, a "hot mess". In high school, she wore the wrong size bra, which gave her double D's a reason to hang down way below her belly button. She had piercings all over her face, her t-shirts were way too small, and she wore Dickie's men's work pants on dates, to parties, to school…a.k.a. IN PUBLIC! If only someone would have stepped in and said, "Hey, why don't you take better care of yourself, you look like S#&t!!" Fortunately, it's never too late to start your friendship with fashion, and eventually, she did just that!

Rayne got her start with fashion as a fit model. Fit models are like live mannequins that give designers suggestions on how to improve the fit, look, and feel of a garment before it goes into production.

Rayne Parvis

Companies like Felina, Tommy Bahama, Sunsets Inc., Anne Cole, and Frederick's of Hollywood, just to name a few, have all hired "for her suggestions", and yes, she has a lot of them.

Before establishing her current company, Style By Rayne, she acquired a B.A. in Cinema Arts & Television Production. Then, for her love of making people laugh, **Rayne** spent a few years packing seats and successfully entertaining at the top comedy clubs in the Los Angeles area...in fishnets, 4 inch heels, a blonde wig, and silly dresses. No really, she did. Her stand-up comic background, as Raynecat, allowed her to share the same stage with such greats as Drew Carey and Dave Attell. Rather than take her talents of spontaneous humor and observation to the next level...**Rayne** found herself drawn to another calling altogether... boosting people's confidence through clothes. She still tells jokes, but only in dressing rooms and people's closets.

Over the years, she developed a keen eye for determining what cuts, designs, and styles will enhance a person's best assets and camouflage a person's least liked body parts. Today, as an image consultant, she possesses tremendous insight into how to fix fashion choices, is a natural at gentle persuasion, and gets to the essence of the person she is re-making. She'll find a way to tell the truth without destroying their self-esteem...and making them laugh at the same time. Rayne walks through this world as if it were her own catwalk, and so will you!

Nicole Drake

Nicole is devoted to empowering and helping others find their "purpose" in life. Her fascination with the inner workings of the mind led her to study Psychology at the College of St. Benedict in Minnesota. She also traveled all over Europe while pursuing her bachelor's degree in London. For a small town girl, big cities were a huge eye opener for her on many levels. Through her travels, education, and relationships she realized how one's self-image can affect the quality of his/her life.

After college she moved to Los Angeles and set out on a quest to find inner happiness. Eventually, through yoga, she reached a deep satisfaction and was determined to share this experience with others. It became her mission to inspire and motivate others to achieve a more successful and balanced life.

Thanks to her soft approach, Nicole is able to prepare clients to substitute the old and outdated for the modern and stylish. As an image consultant, she can walk into a closet, understand what needs to be done, and guide their clients into creating new fabulous visions for themselves.

Today, Rayne and Nicole collaborate in helping people LOOK better and FEEL better than they ever thought they could! They will be saying that phrase over and over, since it's their tag line and they want you to remember it. They have observed countless clients' confidence levels skyrocket as a result of their work with them. Sometimes it just takes a little helping hand or in this case, "hands", to get there. Maybe they haven't been around since the 1800's like Coco Chanel, but that doesn't stop them from sharing their up-to-date opinions, giving suggestions, and changing the world one closet at a time!

Foreword

As a woman who lives in Lulu Lemon and running shoes, writing a foreword for a book about fashion and style may seem a bizarre thing; so let it be known that this bedraggled woman writes this out of love and respect for two stylists who are devoted to, in their words, "making people LOOK better and FEEL better than they ever thought they could".

In my business of life coaching and helping people transform themselves, I understand that real happiness is not found in external circumstances. I also understand that looking your best helps to build confidence and speaks volumes about how you feel about your life.

Although my clients may have good hearts, they often lack the will and know-how to create a style, an attitude, and the best way to present themselves to the world. They need someone to outfit them. So, I send them to Nicole and Rayne who understand the lament of the fashion challenged. They are exceptionally talented ladies who understand outfitting and creating a new style direction to bring out the best in people. They teach how to dress in a way that makes everyone shine from the inside out. It's remarkable to see what a new pair of red pumps or a spiffy tie can do for self-confidence.

Many of my clients are newly single men and women who have lost themselves in life and have forgotten what it is like to feel "sexy" and self-assured. After being married and raising kids, many moms and dads put their self-care on the back burner and don't even realize that they are hiding behind their velour sweatpants and mom jeans. This brings up the questions, "What does your closet say about how you feel about your life?" "Is it filled with uninspired collections of black and white?" "Does it lack color and excitement?" "Is it time for an overhaul?"

Nicole and Rayne to the rescue! The taste-makers and life changers; in charge of keeping us all safe from the fashion blunders that have plagued our lives. They give us the irreplaceable gift of "feeling good". As Giorgio Armani said, "The difference between style and fashion is quality." We must all read their book and take their lead, because looking good is about much more than fashion.

Karen Bayer, Founder, www.NextStage-Coaching.com, Professional Life Coach and Grief Recovery Specialist

www.MeetThePerfectYou.com

Contents

INTRODUCTION

Why the (Bleep) Should I Care?

We are thrilled **you're taking the first fashionable step** to a more polished, professional, and sexier you! An **empowering style isn't just for the famous**, the skinny-minnies, bored housewives, ladies who brunch, teen valley girls, or gold diggers. **It's for everyone** who wants to put his/her best foot forward. We have learned from our many mistakes in the world of fashion, which is one of the reasons why we are so passionate about writing this book. **We know what you're going through.**

The way you look and carry yourself often determines how others will treat you, as it usually is an indication of how you treat yourself. Have you ever looked into a closet full of clothes and said "I have nothing to wear!" or "I wonder if these pants are doing anything for me", or even "I wish there was something I could do to look better… without plastic surgery"? If so, then we are happy that this book has somehow found its way into your hands, onto your Kindle/Nook, or onto your computer screen. Our goal is to help you look better and feel better than you ever thought you could, as well as provide you with a lot of other useful information on how you can present your absolute best!

After reading this book our tips will save you time, money, and help eliminate the overall stress of getting dressed every day. We will guide and **teach you how to purchase items that are right for your body type, skin tone, job, age, and overall lifestyle.** You will learn how to create a balanced appearance for your body shape, how to dress to relay the right message on dates, interviews, and other events. You'll even be able to make a detailed plan for cleaning out your closet.

We want to leave you feeling fabulous, confident, and prepared for wherever the day may take you. This goes for every size, shape, age, and budget. So get ready for us to turn your shopping fears into shopping cheers.

It doesn't matter where you shop. Whether you're at Marshalls, or Neiman Marcus; the current trends have become more free spirited than ever. The options are endless and there are stores available for any budget. With that knowledge, you won't weigh yourself down with the clothes that end up collecting dust and taking up unnecessary space, which ultimately costs you money and time finding what you want to wear. Why not spend that "money and time" on a vacation sipping margaritas on the beach? Many years ago, women didn't have the options we have today. They had one set style and everyone pretty much stuck with that. The **opportunities to look fabulous are now limitless.** Hallelujah!

The following pages **will meticulously take you through the steps towards building a great wardrobe.** Most importantly, stay true to your personality. Every woman has a "catwalker" in them. Find that little girl inside of you that used to play dress-up and get ready to "go get 'em girls!"

CHAPTER 1

Let Your Body Talk: Determine Your Basic Body Type

What Body Type Are You?

Knowing your body type is essential in helping you find the most complementary clothing for your figure. We urge you not to wait until you have the body you someday might have. When you learn how to dress for your <u>current</u> body type, you will likely gain more confidence to either work harder for that dream size or realize you're beautiful just the way you are.

To keep it simple, we use these five shapes: pear, apple, hourglass, rectangle, and extra curvy. Your primary body type may be combined with another secondary one. You will get the best results if you can become familiar with both of them or even all of them. This knowledge will pay off when you discover your own unique body and whenever you may have to help a friend in need. For example, Rayne is a curvy hourglass, but she could also use some helpful tips in the apple section on how to minimize a bigger bust and occasionally her tummy, depending on how many glasses of wine she has consumed.

Most people will encounter a body type change after certain life transitions such as weight loss or weight gain, pregnancy, or just simply the fabulous aging process. Take Nicole, for example. She is a rectangle body type, but the first few months after the birth of her daughter, her body had a few more curves on the bottom half and tummy. During that time period, she took tips from the pear section on how to dress a bigger booty and the apple section on how to hide her tummy.

Fortunately, you don't need be a scientist, have a high IQ, or even be sober to do this. Are you ready to get started? Begin by stripping down into your undergarments. Take a good look at yourself in a full length mirror and study your body shape. Yes, you must take a look at your back side, too.

If you're more voluptuous on the bottom, hips, and thighs, you're most likely a pear. Do you have a little more up top and in the middle than at the bottom? Chances are you're an apple. Do you have ample breasts (natural or enhanced), slimmer waist, and a well-endowed booty, as well? You're an hourglass. Are you thin, no curves, and/or may have characteristics of an athlete? You're a rectangle, also known as straight. (Note: this isn't a reference to your sexual preference... just your body type!) Our goal is to give you the look of a balanced and proportionate body. Still not sure? Keep reading.

The Proud Pear

(Other Pear nicknames: Bell, Triangle, or "A" Shape)

Characteristics:

* Narrow shoulders.

* Small bust.

* Well defined waist.

* Larger hips and thighs (wider than your shoulders).

* Lower body is stronger than your upper body.

* Weight gain most likely shows up in the hips, legs, and thighs.

* Skirts/pants fit loosely at the waistline but tightly on the hips.

Style Tips

A pear's style goal is to balance out the bottom half of the body in relation to the top half. A common mistake pears make is wearing tight body-hugging tops, which actually make the booty, hips, and thighs appear to be larger. As a pear, you want to create an hourglass illusion, accentuating your waist. Direct the attention to your top half. Fun colors, prints, or details all serve the purpose of drawing the eye away from the hip area.

Always try to wear something darker, solid in color, and slimming on the bottom. Darker colored denim, slacks, and knee-length skirts are best. When you keep it simple on the bottom, you have more room to play with your tops and accessories. You can start stocking up your wardrobe with great fitting pants, flared or boot-cut denim, and A-line skirts. Play with colors, prints, and trendier items on top.

When wearing a belt, make sure it's slim and the same color as your pants. A wide belt draws more attention to the area you're trying to minimize. Belt a dress higher up at your waistline, rather than at your hips. Try wearing a fun scarf around your neck, a fabulous necklace, or a great pair of earrings. These items all serve to draw the eye up to your best feature-your face!

How to Balance Your Pear Shape

Tops:

* Make use of jackets. Interesting details around the neckline give more structure to the shoulder area; where you're trying to direct the focus. Choose one that ends below your hips or right above them, not at them.

Structured jacket

* Utilize scoop necks, cowls, and wide open necklines. (These will widen your top half which will then balance with your bottom half).

* Ruffles, puffy, or butterfly sleeves are great choices too.

* Show off your shoulders. The shoulders are a great and sexy part of a woman's body. You can show them off by wearing off-the-shoulder tops that expose one or both shoulders.

* Brocade and taffeta type fabrics work great for adding more dimension to your top half.

Scoop neck
with ruffles

Leopard print
wrapped top

Flowing, V-neck
top with butterfly
sleeves

Bottoms:

* ★ Flat front pants/skirts.

* ★ Slightly flared denim and slacks. A flared leg draws the eye away from your hips and creates a more flattering line for your whole body.

* ★ Skinny jeans will really emphasize your backside. Make sure your top is flowing and drapes nicely, falling below your hips when wearing skinnies.

* ★ Choose materials that hold their form like wool slacks or denim. They flatter and streamline your shape.

* ★ Whatever you wear on the bottom should always be more tailored.

Slightly flared flat
front pants

Waist cinching full
midi-skirt

Empire waist dress

Dresses:

* A-line dresses that skim rather than hug your hips.

* Empire and wrap dresses.

* Strapless dresses that cinch in at your waist and flare out loosely over your hips.

What to Avoid:

* Tight tops.

* Body-hugging bottoms, like super tight skirts.

* Straight, floor-length skirts.

* Sheath dresses.

* Bold, bright colors and attention-grabbing patterns on the bottom.

* High-waisted pants.

* Jeans with too many details, such as extra pockets or embellishments, like rhinestones on your booty pockets.

The Awesome Apple
(Inverted Triangle, Strawberry)

Characteristics:

* Top half is larger than the bottom half.

* Strong upper body.

* May have broad shoulders.

* Average to large bust size.

* Bust is prominent over hips.

* If you gain weight, it goes to your midsection.

* Hips and thighs are narrow.

* Legs are often slender.

Variations: More of a rounded shape, with narrower shoulders, a full bust and waist.

Style Tips

As an apple, you want to emphasize your strong points like your sexy legs, while camouflaging your weaker ones (that stubborn midsection), keeping it all in balance. Opposite of the Pear, stick with the prints on the bottom and solids on top. An eye-catching pencil skirt with a solid top tucked in is a great way to express yourself while also flattering your figure. To create a slimmer waist, tuck in your tops when wearing pencil skirts. This will make your legs look longer and your upper half slimmer.

How to Balance Your Apple Shape

Tops:

* A great bra that supports your bust.

* V-neck jackets that are fully lined
  with a built-in belt that will create
  a nice waistline.

Wrapped sweater with
small flare at bottom

* Blazers should fit perfectly snug on the
  tummy; it will actually act as a tummy
  control when fitted properly.

* Jackets should fall right
  below your hipbone.

* V-neck tops.

* Tunic-style tops and sweaters.

* Shirts that have a small flare or side vent at the bottom.

* Opened tailored button-down shirts.

V-neck jacket with built in belt

Button down tailored shirt

Bottoms:

* Straight pencil skirts. If you're at the office, the shortest your skirt should be is just above the knee. If you're going out for a night on the town, go a little higher!

* A-line skirts also work with your figure, since they flare out from the waist. This type of skirt provides balance and proportion to your upper half.

Mid-rise straight jeans

* Pants with embellished back pockets will give the illusion of a bigger booty.

* Mid-rise denim: straight, boot cut, and slightly flared look great on you!

Dresses:

* Flowing dresses (cinched in with a belt).

* Sheath dresses.

* Empire waist with a slim straight bottom.

Pencil skirt

What to Avoid:

* Double breasted jackets will add more unwanted volume.

* Shoulder pads.

* Shirts with ruffles near the neck line.

* High neck t-shirts and sweaters.

* Tight knits on top, as they show everything, including that extra roll you ate for dinner last night.

Flowing dress cinched in with a belt

* Bold patterns above your waist.

* Anything tight across the chest. Go up a size and have the sides taken in if needed.

* Avoid hanging your purse across your breasts. It will cut them in half.

* Belts at the waist.

* Long necklaces that dangle off the shelf of your breast.

* Pleated fronts, as they will only make your middle look larger.

* Super skinny or tapered leg bottoms, unless you want to look like an ice cream cone.

The Hot Hourglass
(Also known as Cello, "8" Shape, Curvy)

Characteristics:

* Bigger bust.

* Defined waist.

* Curvy hips.

* Possibly a larger behind and shapely legs.

* Proportional and well-balanced.

* Weight gain is proportionate to all of your body, but you may be prone to "love handles" or a little pot belly.

* Your bust and hips are about the same size, and the waist is smaller.

Find out if you're an hourglass by taking a measuring tape and measuring your top and bottom. For example: Rayne has a 39" bust, 28" waist, and 39½" hip. Since her waist is more than nine inches smaller than her hip and chest measurement she is an hourglass. To get your measurements, wrap a measuring tape around your hips and bust by creating a circle (wrap around the biggest part). If you don't want to measure, don't worry about it. There should be plenty of characteristics above to give you a good idea.

Style Tips

Hourglass figures can show off their curves and camouflage their imperfections by knowing how to dress for their shape and choosing the right cuts. Tuck in tops when possible to show off your waist. Wear slightly darker colors to make a full bust or full bottom look

Ultimate Guide to Style: From Drab to Fab!

smaller. When clothes fit properly, any woman can look stunning and she will feel more confident. Embrace your best assets. Don't hide behind poorly fitted clothing. Spend a few more bucks to get your clothing tailored in at the waist, if necessary! A $15 dress can look like a million bucks if it's tailored to fit your body. We salute all the stars who don't give in to Hollywood pressures to be a size "0" and embrace their curvier figures!

How to Emphasize Your Hourglass Shape

Tops:

* A well fitted bra. Since most hourglass figures are well-endowed, a properly fitting bra is a must have wardrobe staple.

V-neck top

* Jackets that create a double "V" that cinch in your waist.

* V-neck or scoop neckline.

* Tailored button up tops with the first few buttons open.

* Belted jackets and wrap style coats.

Double "V"
shaped jacket

Tailored button down
shirt with under-bust
seam and side darts

Pencil skirt (slightly
longer than the apple
pencil skirt)

Bottoms:

* Flat front trousers.

* Boot cut or flared denim.

* For the slender hourglass figures, skinny cut jeans work, too!

* Pencil skirts. (Skirts should come to the middle of the knee cap or slightly shorter.)

Flat front flared trousers

Dresses:

* There are many styles of dresses that work perfectly for hourglass shapes:

* Sheath dresses.

* Wrap dresses (for the curvier hourglass).

* Monochromatic outfits with a slimming belt will slim your figure and balance your body.

* Dresses with ruching.

Body hugging dress with LOTS of ruching

What to Avoid:

* Spaghetti straps (you need thicker straps to balance a full chest).

* Shapeless shirts and skirts. Tops and bottoms that are too big and baggy will only make you look frumpy.

* Trapeze (short, full, shapeless, lots of fabric) dresses.

* Too many details around the bust or bottom area. They will make you look larger and throw off your natural proportions.

Ultimate Guide to Style: From Drab to Fab!

* High neck t-shirts and dresses can make you look like a football player.

The Ravishing Rectangle
(Also Known as Straight, Ruler, Brick, Column, "H" Shape, Athletic)

Characteristics:

* Upper and lower torso is equal in width.

* Average or small bust size.

* Large ribcage.

* Waist and hips are both fairly equal.

* Waist is undefined and body lines are straight.

* Flat bottom and slender legs.

* Most excess weight is distributed evenly.

* People often refer to you as slim and don't believe you when you say you can eat whatever you want and not gain weight.

Variations: Straight body types may also have broad shoulders and a little extra fluff on the tummy. If this is the case, read the 'The Awesome Apple' segment as well, paying extra attention on how to minimize your top half. Overall, you are proportionate with no curves.

Style Tips

You want to create a more feminine and curvy look. You may appear heavier on top, even if your stomach is flat. Your main goal should be to create a waistline, as it will add more width to your upper and lower part — transforming your body into a proportionate hourglass shape. Shiny fabrics, such as sheen, metallics, and silk charmeuse make body parts appear larger and draw attention to them. These fabrics are great for giving the illusion of having more curves. Most models have this body shape, since they are like a hanger for clothes. The greatest benefit to being a rectangle shape is that you can gain weight everywhere and lose it everywhere!

How to Create a Curvier Look

Tops:

* Tops, sweaters, and dresses that cinch at your waistline or right below your bust, such as an empire waist.

* Shirts and tops that have details around the bust area such as ruffles, ruching, sequins and other embellishments.

* Halter tops (avoid if you have broad shoulders).

* Billowy tops.

Wrapped sweater with built in belt

* Jackets and coats that slightly flare out from the waist.

Bottoms:

* Full skirts, such as circle, pleated, trumpet, and A-line styles.

* Lighter colored denims and slacks.

* Corduroy pants add texture and curves.

* Wide leg bottoms; the flare hem will give the illusion that you have hips.

Wide leg trousers

* Skinny jeans.

| Billowy top (a great shirt to camouflage a bigger tummy too) | Halter top | Curve enhancing pleated skirt | Skinny jeans |

Dresses:

* Sheath dresses create curves in all the right places.

* Halter dresses that show off your sexy shoulders. This is not recommended for broad shoulders.

* Strapless dresses that tightly hug your body and go down to just above the knee.

* Wrap dresses, which will give the illusion of more curves.

* Asymmetrical cuts with ruching will give you extra curves.

Sheath dress

What to Avoid:

* Vertical patterns and lines. These tend to make you appear thin and lanky.

* Clingy, square, and tightly fitted tops.

* Short cropped jackets that end at your waist.

* Straight cut denim will only emphasize your straight figure.

Extra Curvy Pointers
(Also known as Diamond, Oval, Plus Size)

If you have a little more *cushion for the pushin'*, you don't need to worry about trends as much as selecting clothing and styles that have proven to give you the best body shape. If you're a size 16 plus, we consider you extra curvy and you will benefit most by shopping in the plus size section. There are so many retailers that cater to voluptuous women. With the right cuts and style, you will look stunning!

You want to steer away from anything boxy, not fitted, or too tight. Horizontal stripes aren't your friend. We are truly sorry to break it to you, but all black does not make you look slimmer. It gives off an aggressive, non-feminine aura. In addition to the following tips read; the above Pear, Apple, and Hourglass sections. For example, you may be an extra curvy pear with a heavy mid-section. So you will want to follow the pear and apple midsection suggestions along with these tips.

Pick Out:
- ★ Choosing darker hues from your color palette will make you appear slimmer.
- ★ Medium size designs and patterns that run vertically.
- ★ Monochromatic outfits.
- ★ Structured jackets with a slight flare at the waist.
- ★ Choose long, lean, non-boxy, quarter length coats in classic colors (navy, camel, black) to keep warm, rather than bulky sweaters.

* V-neck lines.

* Wrap, empire, sheath, and A-line dresses.

* Straight.

What to Avoid:

* Ruffles will add inches to you; so no ruffles anywhere.

* Horizontal stripes.

* Huge prints-you don't want to look like you're wearing a comforter or a couch.

* Shiny fabrics.

* Wide belts.

Wrap dress

Perfectly Petite Pointers

If you're shorter than 5'4", we consider you petite. All the body shapes mentioned above can come in petite. Combine your body shape tips with these suggestions.

You want to appear longer and leaner; who doesn't? The perfect fit is extra important for you. If you wear clothes that are too long or too baggy, it will look like you're playing dress-up in your mom's clothes. You want to go with more exotic colors rather than primary

"Krisa coated drape jacket and Nation LTD Oregon Tee are currently my favorite go to looks. These drape the mid-section rather than hug my problem area. I just can't seem to say "no" to those big burritos!"

—Carla Shammas, friend and Operations Manager

colors. Exotic colors such as gold, peach, or ocean blue will provide an air of sophistication for you. Stay away from regular t-shirts, sweatshirts, and hoodies. These will make you look childish and boyish. Avoid bulky sweaters and big patterns, as these will swallow you up. Stick to slim and straight fitted bottoms and dresses, small prints and preferably, above or on the knee-length hemlines!

Pick Out:

* If you're slender: lighter colors from your color palette, since these will automatically make you appear bigger.

* If you're curvy: stick with the darker colors.

* A cropped blazer, rather than a jean jacket.

* Clothes with vertical lines, piping, and/or seams will make you look taller.

* High-waist pants and skirts make your legs appear longer.

* Body hugging dresses that fall just below the knee will give you an alluring womanly look.

* Comfortable everyday heels. Brands like Cole Haan, Naturalizer, and Sofft Shoe create amazing, all day wearable shoes.

What to Avoid:

* Horizontal stripes.

* Capri pants.

* Long unshapely shirts. All tops should fall right below or at your hips.

* Tight mini-skirts.

Keep in mind that these tips are simply <u>guidelines</u>. We all have to begin somewhere in order to dress in a flattering and fab combination of ensembles. Once you get the hang of it, you will begin to view your body and fashion in a whole new way! Knowing what styles, colors, and cuts to look for will make shopping less time consuming, less confusing, and more fun. We will dig deeper into how to shop in Chapter 11.

Ask yourself these questions, "Does this outfit balance my shape? Does it draw attention to my best assets? Will it downplay my problem areas? Does this pattern match my frame? Did I create a waist?". If you answer yes to these questions, then you're dressing for your specific body type.

Note: There is nothing wrong with a size "0", as long as you are meant to be that way. If you are starving yourself, working out five hours a day, and taking diet pills, then we hate to break it to you… maybe you aren't meant to be a size "0". Your health comes first. Being in the modeling industry, we have both witnessed women going to extremes to be super skinny. They ended up damaging their bodies, were mental cases, and lost a lot of friends. Sorry, but we get bitchy if we are hungry. Please seek professional help if you need it and please don't let this happen to you.

Ultimate Guide to Style: From Drab to Fab!

CHAPTER 2

Make a Statement: Determine Your Style Personality

We are like snowflakes...beautiful, unique, and no two are alike! Yes, we know, twins may come close, but even <u>they</u> have different preferences and personalities. Your wardrobe portrays a REFLECTION of you. We wouldn't want to categorize any woman into a style "stereotype", because our style is often affected by our ever-changing moods, but we all tend to have one dominant personality. It's our natural instinct to choose a particular type of clothing, but due to trends, bargains, budget, time issues, friends, media, and whatever is on the mannequin, we often buy clothes that don't match our true inner selves.

"Not to compare you fabulous ladies to dogs, but I have to share this story as an example. I volunteer for an animal shelter. We style the homeless dogs in bandanas, collars, and bows to make them look ADORABLE so people will adopt them. One day a volunteer put a spiked black collar on a white, blue eyed pitbull named Sadie. You may think that pitbulls belong in spiked collars, as they are known to be aggressive, rough, and sad to say, fighting dogs. However, Sadie was the sweetest little angel. She acted like a lap dog, gave a million kisses, and just wanted to cuddle. If you judged her by her collar, you would think the former, she was going to be snarly and mean. I traded Sadie's collar for a pink-flowered bandana that I tied in a pretty feminine bow. Sadie's outer adornment now matched her warm and friendly personality! She was being misrepresented in the spiked collar." —*Rayne*

Before (pictured left), Sadie was not styled to fit her personality. I switched out the spike collar for the bow (right) and TA-DA...Sadie was now representing her personality!

Are you misrepresenting yourself like Sadie was? Are you dressing like you're someone else? Are you sweet and demure, but try to "rock out" over-the-knee boots with ripped jeans and a mesh top? Does that entirely black outfit match your cheery and vivacious outlook on life? Are you neat and articulate at your job, but your wardrobe is sloppy? By the way, yes, Sadie was adopted!

Ultimate Guide to Style: From Drab to Fab!

Try this. Circle the letters in the following questionnaire to help you determine your style personality. If you find that more than one answer works, do your best to choose just one. If you have a closet full of sweatpants and t-shirts, take the time to go through style magazines or think of a celebrity whose style you admire, and answer the questions based on how you would like to see yourself.

How Would You Describe Your Overall Look?

a. Eclectic and fun with an edge.

b. Trendy, glamorous, and up to date.

c. Feminine with a vintage vibe.

d. Polished and always put together.

e. Casual and effortless.

What Do You Wear to Work?

a. Basic pieces with a hint of my wild side.

b. Head-to-toe designer.

c. Ladylike dresses in light colors.

d. Tailored suits, tailored suits, and more tailored suits.

e. Plain sweaters, t-shirts paired with comfortable jeans/ slacks, and a blazer for meetings.

How Would You Describe Your Shoe Collection?

a. Wild and bright with elements of complete surprise.

b. Expensive and hot.

c. Soft pastels and feminine florals.

d. Basic and sophisticated, in timeless styles.

e. Comfortable.

What Kind Of Jewelry Do You Wear?

a. Pieces that are unique, fun, and that resemble my favorite things (cats, strawberries, music, favorite colors).

b. Big, bold, and lots of it.

c. Dainty and soft.

d. Sophisticated and elegant; love the classic diamond studs.

e. Small earrings on a special occasion or none at all.

How Would You Describe Your Make-Up Routine?

a. I focus on one feature (lips, eyes, or cheeks) and make it pop.

b. I change it up with my mood.

c. Natural and basic.

d. Precise and consistent.

e. I barely wear make-up.

My Friends Would Say I Am:

a. Gregarious, creative, a little rebellious.

b. Loyal, family oriented, slight perfectionist.

c. Sweet, peace-maker who is soft spoken.

d. Trustworthy.

e. Down to earth.

Tally It Up, Ladies!

Count how many times you circled a-e and tally it here:

a. _____   c. _____   e. _____

b. _____   d. _____

Ultimate Guide to Style: From Drab to Fab!

If You Have:

Mostly a's:

You're a *Creative*. You're a woman who chooses a wardrobe that fits you. You're drawn to bold pieces and like to add something special and fun to each outfit. You find great pleasure going to thrift shops and discount stores looking for a one-of-a-kind piece at a bargain. It's rare for you to throw anything out, since you know you will wear it at some point, even if it needs some work. You will put pieces together that others would never dream of doing.

You have an eye for mixing thrift store finds with modern looks. You're the one personality who can look classic, artsy, romantic, and fun all in one outfit. Your personality is like your wardrobe: colorful and fun. Many things in your life reflect your love, creativity, and passion.

Mostly b's:

You're a *Dramatic Fashionista*. You're a woman who is always up to date and usually has the endless budget to maintain it. You enjoy the process of getting ready from start to finish. Dress to the nines EVERY time.

You rarely leave the house without face of make-up perfection and your hair is straightened or perfectly curled with extensions. Your many handbags are all top notch designers. Your friends often comment on your intense, bold and bright style and ask you "Is that new?" and "Where did you get it?". You're very loyal and fortunately for them, you don't mind sharing your designer items with your pals.

Mostly c's:

You're a *Romantic*. You're a woman who chooses a wardrobe that reflects your humble lifestyle. You carry yourself in a happy and carefree way. You want your clothes to be soft and feminine. You have a unique knack for making your laid back wardrobe of patterns, fringes, and lace with delicate details look effortless, although it has been well-planned.

Your demeanor is like your wardrobe: airy, soft, and peaceful. Your friends can always depend on your shoulder to cry on.

Mostly d's:

You're *Classically Chic*. You're a woman who always looks sophisticated and well put together. You wear traditional pieces of clothing as a foundation, but will add a beautiful eye-catching piece of jewelry and classic designer handbag. Your style is timeless. You have a beautifully structured wardrobe of tailored pieces that will last for years to come.

You can mix and match most of your clothes, since they are usually basic colors. Outfits are like your desk, well organized and coordinated. You like to stay understated, yet chic. Your shoes are polished and perfect. You're reliable, punctual, and will go out of your way for loved ones.

Mostly e's:

You're a *Minimalist*. You're a woman who chooses a wardrobe that reflects your modest lifestyle. Clothing is soft, easy to care for, and comfortable. You may even dread dressing up for a special occasion. You often variations of same things. Your standard outfit is jeans, flat shoes, and a sweater or t-shirt.

You have a big heart and are often focused on bigger worldly problems, rather than finding the perfect outfit or the right shoe. Your denim should be amazing so that you stay looking hot, but natural. If you find a perfect fitting t-shirt or sweater, you should buy more than one in your color palette. Colors will keep you looking fresh and up to date. This can be the deal breaker between looking sloppy and casually cool.

FIZZLIN' and SIZZLIN' Style Personality

If you have a mixture of answers, then your wardrobe is fizzlin' and needs careful investigation. Ask yourself, what style most represents you? For those of you starting from scratch, think about what style gets you excited. Go through magazines and tear out pictures of clothes, bags, and shoes that you can see yourself in. Make a "my style" vision board by pasting or taping all your "wish I had" items on a cardboard, then hang it by your closet to inspire the best dressed you!

If you are wondering, the style personality that Rayne embodies is generally *Creative* and Nicole is *Classically Chic*. During the summer, for example, they both may reflect their *romantic* side with flowing dresses. They differ in that Nicole would choose a neutral colored t-strap sandal and simple jewelry to keep it sophisticated and classic. In contrast, Rayne would wear a bright colored t-strap sandal, bold earrings, and a funky cat ring to keep it fun and true to her personality. Once you get the hang of dressing like you, you won't be fizzlin' and you will be…sizzlin'!

Ultimate Guide to Style: From Drab to Fab!

CHAPTER 3

We See Your True Colors: How to Choose Colors to Flatter Your Face

How amazing were the 80's?! Heavy metal bands like Guns N' Roses and Motley Crue, the hepatitis vaccine, Apple's Macintosh, CD-ROM, the artificial human heart, DNA fingerprinting, fashion icons like Madonna, and most importantly, *Color Me Beautiful's* beauty regimen on how to look younger by determining your color palette.

Color can make a huge difference in the way we look and feel. For example, most of us love wearing the color black. We think that black is sexy, sophisticated, makes us look thinner, and is a great "go to" basic color. Ironically, black is often <u>not</u> a great choice. If you have a winter color palette, you're in luck. If you're wondering what we mean by that, keep on reading.

To help you understand how you can use color to your advantage in your everyday life, we thought it would be great for you to hear it from the fabulous color expert herself, Audessa Siccardi. We have tried, tested, and received training from her on how your choice of color can affect your overall appearance. Here is what she has to say:

Improve Your Image. Improve Your World.

"The colors people wear have a true impact on how we perceive them. Right or wrong, we feel attracted, neutral or repelled."

You and Color

Have you ever noticed someone walk into a room and it seems as if everyone is drawn to him or her? You may not be sure of the reason. Often, this is because both confidence and color attract. Just imagine our world without color; drab, dull and boring; black, white or gray. With color, our world shines, sparkles, and becomes more alive!

On the contrary, when you wear colors that are unsuited for you, you can appear washed out, pale, or even sickly. If you have had a full night's rest and your friends or co-workers comment, "You look tired today," it may simply be due to a poor color selection in your wardrobe. The most important area where color makes the greatest impact is near your face, particularly your neckline.

Warm Colors vs. Cool Colors

How do you know whether warm or cool colors look best on you? It's based on your skin tone, eye color and natural hair color, as well as your current hair color. A general rule of thumb is that warm colors look good on warm toned skin, and cool colors flatter cool toned skin.

Are you wondering which colors are cool and which ones are warm? Both warm and cool colors can be found in nature. Imagine the rich warm reds, oranges, and golden yellows of a beautiful sunset. Now think of the earth; the grassy or muddy greens, the rich brown dirt and soft, beige sand. Colors of our sun and earth represent warm colors.

Plain sweaters, t-shirts paired with comfortable jeans/slacks, and a blazer for meetings. For cool colors, picture the sky with its whites, grays and various hues of blue, even the charcoal gray and black clouds. Now imagine the ocean, from the clear turquoise waters to the deep indigo seas. The colors of our sky and ocean represent cool colors.

Skin Tone

Skin tones are warm, cool, or neutral, just like colors. Warm skin tones can vary from yellow to peach, beige to warm brown, reddish-brown to deep brown, and the many shades in between. Cool skin tones can be white, pink, pinkish-red, deep dark brown, or black. These represent the majority of skin types, yet some of us actually fall into the neutral category. To determine which clothing colors will enhance your skin tone, your eye color and hair color must also be considered.

Eye Color

In color analysis, I have found that most people who have gold or amber tones in their eyes belong in the warm color category. You may have flecks of gold, specks of amber, or even just an overall amber glow in your eyes. Hazel or greenish-brown eyes and golden brown eyes also belong to this group.

In contrast, people who have no gold or amber in their eyes generally seem to look best in colors from the cool color palettes. Typically, this means your eyes are blue, blue-gray, clear green (not muddy green or hazel), or sometimes dark brown. There are some people who have a yellow ring around their pupils or even a single golden spot in one eye. If their skin tone is warm, I have found they belong in the warm classification.

Hair Color

Another step to finding the perfect colors for your wardrobe is by coordinating them with your hair color. What was your hair color when you were 12 years old? That is, of course, assuming it was not dyed at that time. Your natural hair color is characteristically in balance with your skin tone and eye color. Once you dye your hair, you open up the possibility of looking unnatural or out of balance with your natural eye color and skin tone. Also, if you make a change that is radically different, it may require you to reduce the selection of seasonal colors in your personal color palette, in order to still look your best.

If you have been trying to determine whether you're warm or cool based on your skin tone, eye color and hair color, you may discover your results are: skin tone warm, eyes cool, hair warm OR skin cool, eyes cool, hair warm. This isn't out of the ordinary.

Your Seasonal Colors

What do seasonal colors represent? They are categorized into nature's four seasons: spring, summer, autumn, and winter. During spring, we see fresh, new green grass and colorful blooming flowers. Summer is a good time to enjoy turquoise waters, sandy beaches, and beautiful blue skies. Autumn's colors boast a burst of colorful yellow, orange, and red falling leaves, along with a harvest of vibrant pumpkins, squash, and golden grains. As we transition to winter, we experience striking white snow and black night skies. Most people fall into these four seasonal color groups.

"Wow! That's a lot of colorful information. How do we determine our season?" —*Ladies*

Personal Color Analysis

If your hair is naturally blond or ash in color and you have blue eyes and a pale or pinkish skin tone, it's likely that summer colors look best on you.

Winter's cool colors often look fabulous on men or women with pale skin and black hair. However, it also depends on what shade of blue, brown, or green eyes they have. Others with medium to dark skin, brown hair and brown eyes without any amber tones are also likely to be classified as a winter.

You may be one of those fortunate people designated as a spring and have the joy of wearing the greatest variety of colors of any other seasonal group. Springs typically have warm-toned skin which is light to medium in color. Their eyes may have an amber tone like hazel, clear blue or green. Hair color can vary from dirty blond to a variety of browns, reds, or grays.

Autumn colors look terrific on people with hazel or green eyes and medium to dark, warm toned skin. If you have amber eyes, medium to dark warm toned skin and brown or reddish hair, the autumn color palette will complement your natural beauty.

The Psychology of Color

Some colors may make you appear "lovely" or "trustworthy", while others make you seem "fun" or "sexy". The individual impact of color from one person to another is distinctive. Combining the right colors together will create a "Wow!" impact.

Color selections are also based on your personality and whether you're introverted or extroverted. After all, it would not make sense to suggest that an extremely shy, quiet woman wear a bold, hot pink dress to an event. Nor would I recommend that a flashy, fun, outgoing man wear beige from head to toe. Each individual's level of comfort and special style should be carefully considered.

Take Action to Look Your Absolute Best

Your color palette can be utilized for years, sometimes even decades. Although, when we age, often our skin pales and our hair becomes lighter, gray or white. This is the time to reevaluate your wardrobe colors and possible move to a different color palette with lighter tones.

If you're at all unsure as to which color palette is the right one for you, find a professional color expert. Wait, no, you have just found me! I look forward to meeting with you and helping you. Remember, once you do it right with color, you will improve your image and improve your world.

By Audessa Siccardi Copyright 2012

Thank you, Audessa! We really appreciate your fantastic guidelines on color. You're truly a gem! Below you can find a few tips on how to choose your "wow" colors.

Choose Colors to Flatter Your Skin Tone

Winters look striking in colors that are deep, sharp, and clear. White, black, blue, red, and a shocking pink will all go well with winter complexions. For lighter colors, wear icy bold tones rather than pastels. Avoid subdued tones like beige and gold. As you age, go with deep purples and blues rather than black and red.

Springs can wear warm colors, like off-white, dark peach, golden yellow and golden brown, teal, sorbet, and violet. Avoid winter colors around your face.

Summers options include pastels and soft neutrals with rose and blue undertones. Lavender, plum, rose-brown, and soft blue accommodate summers well while black and orange do not.

Autumns should select colors with golden undertones, like camel, beige, orange, gold, grass greens, and dark brown. Avoid colors with blue tones, like navy blue, and black.

One color that looks amazing on every season is: drum rolls please, PERIWINKLE!

Five Color Combinations to Avoid

"Sorry, I have to get this off my double D chest and into this chapter and give you a few color combinations that drive me NUTS. In my opinion, one of the reasons why most of us love holidays so much is due to the change of attire, mood, and scenery. I love being festive, but when the holidays are over these combinations are no longer aesthetically attractive. If you show up at a summer barbecue wearing brown, burgundy, and orange, you may be mistaken for a turkey and thrown straight on the barbecue. I am exaggerating, but you get the picture.

It's best to avoid these color combos when they are not in the holiday season:

1. Brown, burgundy, orange: reminds me of a
   Thanksgiving tablecloth.

2. Red, white, gold jewelry: reminds me of a Christmas ornament.

3. Red, white, with black boots: reminds me of Santa's helpers.

4. Orange and black: reminds me of Halloween decorations.

5. All green with black belt: reminds me of a leprechaun.

Bonus tip: "I would also stay away from the green top and brown bottom combo, unless you enjoy looking like a tree. Last, but not least, black and yellow turns you into a buzzing bumble bee. I apologize for any turkey feathers that I may ruffle. Underneath my shield of humor, I am a bundle of love!" —*Rayne*

Ultimate Guide to Style: From Drab to Fab!

CHAPTER 4

Discussing the Delicates: Putting Your Panties and Bras to Work for You

Give yourself the gift of a proper fitting "foundation". Your bras, panties, and shapewear are the "underlying" groundwork. Think of your underwear like the blueprint for the Eiffel Tower. It's the foundation to one of the most beautiful and astonishing sights in the world. Why shouldn't your body be viewed as one of the Seven Wonders of the World? No, we aren't kidding. We want you to view yourself as an amazing piece of work!

You can be wearing a $2,000 dress, but it can look awful and cheap if you're wearing the wrong underwear. In comparison, you can have on a $50 dress and look like a million bucks due to the right bra and panties. Your underwear can help you create the look of the body you always dreamed of having. A great bra can lift, add a few cup sizes, or minimize. The right underwear can nip, tuck, or smooth. The perfect shapewear can do it all! You will hold your head up high knowing that you have got secret weapons working for you.

As far as bra size, we aren't going to teach you how to determine that; you need to be professionally fitted. Department stores like Macy's, Victoria's Secret, and Bloomingdale's all have trained staff that can help you accurately determine your bra size. Our goal is to give you a balanced and supportive feel with the look of an hourglass shape. Keep reading for all your lifting, enhancing, minimizing, and slimming needs.

The BOOBIES

According to numerous blog postings, lingerie company studies, and surveys, 75-85% of women are wearing the wrong size bras. That is nearly every woman. Individually, our breasts can change drastically depending on that time of the month, pregnancy, or weight fluctuation. It gets complicated and on top of that, most women's breasts aren't even symmetrical. Here are some signs that you're wearing the wrong sized bra:

Wire Coming Off Your Body

Look at the front center of your bra. If the wire is not lying flat on your sternum, it means your cups are too small. Some other things to consider are the size of the straps and the band width. If you have bigger breasts, you will most likely need the extra support that comes with a thicker padded strap and at least three hook clasps for the band. If you have small or average sized breasts, you can get away with skinnier straps and two hooks should be enough to keep your boobies looking perky and peppy.

Double Bubble

You're wearing a cup size that is too small if there is any extra "boobie" coming out of the bra.

Loosey Goosey

If there is any wrinkling in the fabric, or if you can fit more than two fingers underneath and pull the bra more than an inch away from your body, your bra is too big. Look at your bra from the back; the band shouldn't be riding up.

Pokey Little Wire

If your bra has an underwire, lift your arm up and feel where the underwire ends. The underwire should completely encompass your "girls". If the wire is poking the breast tissue, your cup is too small. The wire should stop right underneath your armpit where your breast begins.

"Being a fit model for many years, I have been taught by designers how to properly fit in a bra. After you have put on the bra, you must jiggle the wires in place, bend over, and then let your breast tissue fall into the cup. This allows the bra to do the work and it makes sure your breasts are in the right place." —*Rayne*

Tips for Full Figures

We advise our clients with sizes D, DD, F, and so on to purchase Frederick's of Hollywood's VA VA VOOM bra. It does wonders for our "twins". The bra gives them an amazing flattering shape. The padded thick strap doesn't dig into the shoulders. The soft molded cups are very sturdy and it can endure a hundred or more washes before needing to be replaced. "I was hired by Frederick's of Hollywood to help get the best fit, therefore I can strongly support (get it? SUPPORT?) this bra. In addition, its satin feel and sleek look is so sexy!" —*Rayne*

Another tip to consider is the center front closure. The two wires should be "kissing" aka touching. This is something that we tell all our clients. This kissing of the wire keeps "the girls" in the center. Some bras will have a half inch separation. This makes the breasts move further out. The goal is to keep the breast tissue in and controlled.

For a minimizer bra, we recommend Wacoal. Wacoal bras have an amazing quality, nice shape, and they last forever. However, be careful with minimizers. You don't want to look like you have a uni-boob. Minimizers compact and smoosh all the tissue up against you. Be careful not to create an extra set of boobs coming out of your armpits. It's best to get a good supportive bra that gives you a lift, rather than a smoosh.

A helpful hint to all our big busted bosom buddies is to stand up straight and tall. A great posture will make you look 10 pounds thinner and you will look so much more confident.

If you're looking for a strapless bra or corset, you will need to go down a band size and up a cup size. For example, I normally wear a 34DD, so I will need to purchase a 32DDD. The weight of the breasts is so heavy that the strapless bras will slide down the body if you don't have a tighter band to hold "the girls" in place. —*Rayne*

Colors to Buy

Purchase nude and black ones. Nude is the best, because it rarely shows up through clothing. Black can be worn under darker colors. If you're like us, you have made the mistake of buying too many bras with bright patterns and crazy colors, simply because they were on sale. The problem with these bras is that they always seem to show through your clothes, so you rarely wear them.

Bra Styles

Seamless Bras – These give a smooth fitted shape and look by using a stretch or molded cup.

Push-up – These bras add cleavage by pushing the breasts together, which can add up to a cup size…hence "push up".

Padded Push-up – Made with pads, gel, or water inserts. The inserts can be removable and most importantly, add a cup size or two. These are great for small busted women and more convenient than a boob job!

Demi – Exposes the top portion of the breast and gives off a look of seduction with less support. This bra is ideal for low cut shirts, blouses, and dresses. Not recommended for all-day wear or full figures.

Balconette – A popular exotic lingerie bra, also known as a balcony bra, provides less breast coverage and support than the demi bra. These bras work great with lower cut necklines on blouses, tops, sweaters, and dresses, because of their cleavage enhancing effects. Definitely not recommended for all-day wear or full figures.

Racerback – Work great under summer tank tops and sleeveless shirts. The bra straps disappear from view by curving toward the shoulder blades. The bra is very comfortable and a wise choice for women with narrow shoulders.

T- Shirt Bra – This very popular bra is made to be almost entirely invisible under tight fitted clothing.

Backless – These are designed to be worn under strapless, backless halter dresses and styles with a plunging neckline. To prevent slippage, an inner line of silicone adhesive works wonders. (This is NOT recommended for full busts for obvious reasons).

Adhesive Bras – Supported by adjustable adhesive cups that form to the breasts. These are ONLY for small breasts.

Full Figure – The name sums it up. These bras tend to have fuller coverage, more clasps in the back and thicker shoulder straps, providing more support.

Minimizer – Designed specifically for the full breasted women and those who want to give the illusion of a smaller bust line.

The BOTTOMS

Like your bras, black and nude are the most wearable colors. If you stick to these colors, you will always be wearing a matching bra and panty set. How sexy! However, we recommend having at least one red, pink lace, or polka-dot bra and panty set to spice up your love life, when you're in a playful mood, or to change it up a bit.

The most important tip for wearing undies is to make sure there are NO VISIBLE PANTY LINES, a.k.a. VPL's! It doesn't matter what size or shape you happen to be. Panty lines aren't only unattractive and noticeable, but they also take away from the beauty of your figure flattering clothing. Panty lines just look sloppy.

Our personal favorite panty pick is the thong, otherwise known as the g-string. Yes, thongs get a bad rap, but think about it, they have no VPL's. If something is going to ride up your rear all day, why not a little piece of string rather than a bunch of fabric? Trust us on this one. If you have never worn them, please try them. We guarantee you will change your mind and have a new friendship and adoration for thongs.

If there are just no if's, and's or BUTT's about you wearing a thong, we respect your preference for full booty underwear. Look for underwear by the name of "raw edge" or seamless. These will give you a nice smooth look and will cover your booty without the elastic hugging all over your delicate parts. We have heard it through the grapevine that tight fitting elastic can trigger cellulite. Who wants more of that? Not us.

Smoothing Shapewear

Shapewear is a must for dresses. Shapewear gives a more toned and smooth appearance to any flaws you may have. It can make you look 10 pounds thinner, as well as enhance your God-given shape. No matter if you're a size 2 or a size 18, shapewear is your friend.

The most universal brand is Spanx. Kim Kardashian is a huge promoter and fan of Spanx. Even if you don't care much for Kim Kardashian, you can see what shapewear has done for her body. Another brand that offers many different styles is Classic Shapewear.

We prefer the boy short shapewear when wearing skirts. The skirt shapewear is rarely the right length and it bunches up. Another great tip is to make sure the leg and waistband grips without cutting into your skin. Slimming tank tops can also be purchased to wear under sweaters and shirts for women who have extra love handles.

For your undergarments that are torn, tattered, or worse, stained... toss them. Yes, we have "period panties" too, but they are black. Shopping isn't like it was ten years ago. There are many choices of comfortable and unique "delicates" available today. Wear sexy undergarments, even if you're the only one who knows or sees them. They will give you a boost of self-confidence and a reason to mischievously smile. People will notice and may find you intriguing. Now would be a great time to go get your secret weapons, ladies. Why wait?

Note: We left out the sexy edible undies and pasties for obvious reasons. These do nothing for the actual overall look of your body.

> "Remember ladies, just because you are married or in a relationship, don't trade in your sexy lingerie for sweat pants and a t-shirt with a beer slogan across the chest. Something silky and feminine is a much better way to keep them happy and interested."
>
> —Marla Martenson, friend, match-maker, and author of *Excuse Me Your Soul Mate Is Waiting*

CHAPTER 5

Dating Dilemmas: Wear This, Not That on Dates and Why

If you're single and dating, you only get one shot at making a first impression. Let's make it an unforgettable one. We know you may be thinking, "If they get to know the real me, it shouldn't matter what I wear." We've got news for you! If you show up looking like you just raided the Walmart sales rack, wearing the same dress you wore when you rang in the new millennium or wearing inappropriate attire for the date, you will most likely be dismissed as a potential mate faster than you can spell Mississippi. (We hope that did not come off as offensive.) Married ladies, please read this chapter also. One important key to a long happy marriage is keeping up with your appearance.

When dressing for a date, give off the same vibe as the amazing person you want to attract. Portraying yourself in a demure fashion, no matter what the occasion, will only increase your chances of attracting love. If you want to be treated like a lady, dress like one. Then, if you have chemistry and your date is smart and commitment worthy, he will take the time to get to know you. If you want to attract a physically fit man, be fit yourself. Do yourself a favor and buy a gym membership. Do you want to be someone's wife? Ask yourself: "Do I look like a nice bride or a floozy one-night stand?" Your fashion choices should work for you, not against you.

It's vitally important to find out where you will be going and research it before you make any wardrobe decisions for the date. Take notes and learn from some of our funny mishaps, even though they were not so funny at the time. We can laugh at them now, especially because it turns out that we can help so many other women avoid the same mistakes. Let's have some fun and get ready for the "what to WEAR to WHERE"!

Outdoor Beautiful Daytime Dates

Imagine a scenario where he has planned a long walk in the park so his dog can play, but you show up wearing a silk dress and your brand new suede pumps that aren't broken in yet. As you walk onto the grass, your heels start digging into the dirt and you start to sweat. Not our idea of a good time. If this type of impromptu date dilemma happens to you, sit in the shade and take off your heels. Your date will be pleasantly surprised when you reveal your perfect pedicure.

If you're going to see a sports game or a similar event, it could result in an embarrassing fall and scab to the knee when wearing high heels or flip flops. Falling down the bleachers and showing everybody your fanny would be funny, but pretty painful. There will probably be a lot of walking and he isn't going to be happy with you taking itty bitty steps. You want to enjoy yourself and not be bogged down by your fashion choices. What about flat sandals with straps? If you don't mind going home with ketchup and French fries stuck in between your toes, then go for it!

"I made the mistake of showing up to play golf in sexy exercise attire that showed off my midriff. Not a smart choice on my part for a fancy country club. Not only did I turn a few shades of red from embarrassment after being asked to change, but then I proceeded to drive the golf cart over the putting green practice area! I couldn't figure out how to put the darn thing in reverse. Oh, did I mention that I had just met my date's dad for the first time and he was a witness to all of this? Fortunately for me, they got past it, and we dated for quite some time. I'm pretty sure this story continues to get a laugh every time it's told." —*Nicole*

Barbecue Dates

"My date at the time said we were going to a birthday party and the invitation said it was at the "Alcott House". I didn't bother reading the rest of the invitation. One thing I did know is Jeannie Mai, the host of How Do I Look was going to be there and I wanted to look like I knew a thing or two about fashion. I decided I couldn't go wrong by wearing a bright electric snakeskin print dress and my

4 inch heels. I figured the restaurant would be dark and I could get away with wearing my neon dress. It was her stylist's birthday, and I was pretty confident that everyone else there would be standing in 5 inch high heels too.

Well, I was wrong. The "Alcott House" was just that, a person's house on Alcott Street. I arrived at the barbecue. Most of the women were tiny beautiful Asians, standing around 5 feet tall in sandals and maxi dresses. If I had known, I would've been wearing the same attire. I mean, it was a barbecue. Not only was I a whopping 6'2" in heels, which made me over a foot taller than everyone else, including the men, but my dress was incredibly blinding. I even came close to falling a few times because my heels kept getting caught in the crevices of the porch. Although, the day wasn't a complete disaster, I ended up chatting with my favorite TV stylist, Jeannie Mai! Ever since that day, I carry a pair of fold-a-flats in my purse and ask questions regarding the dress attire." —*Rayne*

PS. Jeannie Mai is as sweet as she is on TV.

Two Reasons Why Maxi Dresses are Our "Pick" for Barbecue Attire:

1. They are comfortable whether you're sitting on a lawn chair, a bench, or on the grass.
2. You can eat as much as you want! We both enjoy good wine and veggie burgers. If we wear jeans, we have to unbutton the top button.

Monochromatic maxi-dress

With a maxi dress, there's more room to grow! Nicole wore them all the time when she was pregnant. They look great on every BODY.

If you have a summer barbecue to attend, and you feel that you may eat or drink a little too much, our suggestion is to put on a lightweight, cropped cotton tee over your maxi dress. Add some stack-able bracelets, and a big cocktail ring. All these things will draw attention away from the stomach area, unless maybe, you're expecting next month.

More Clothing Options for Hot Weather Events:

Tops:

* Light-weight cotton t-shirts or tanks in complementing colors.

* Casual jackets or cardigans, just in case it gets cold at night. You can also use them to sit on as sometimes the seats can be dirty, or give you weird indents on your skin if you're wearing shorts.

Bottoms:

* Perfect fitting tight jeans, if it's not too hot.
* Jean shorts.
* Maxi skirts.

Dresses:

* Sun dresses (knee length or a little shorter).
* Maxi dresses.

Shoes:

- ∗ T-strap sandals or wedges if you want a little height (not for a sports game).

- ∗ Fashionable slip-ons or ballet flats.

- ∗ Flat boots (ankle length).

Quick make-up tip: Make-up for the daytime shouldn't be overdone. Prepare to be hot and in the sun, which means the more make-up you wear, the more disastrous it can be. Imagine having runny mascara, melting cover-up, and red lipstick all over the place. This is literally a HOT MESS.

We Recommend:

- ∗ Tinted moisturizer for cover-up.

- ∗ Concealer.

- ∗ Translucent powder.

- ∗ Mascara.

- ∗ Light colored blush.

- ∗ Nude colored lip gloss. That's it!

Dinner and Drinks

Our client Julie, a 46 year old single woman, needed a date pick-me-up. Covered head to toe in a masculine drab outfit isn't going to grab a potential life partner's attention. She was wearing baggy jeans, masculine boots, and a sweater. We have found through our own experiences and our clients' feedback that a nice dress and heels will get an engine roaring and your confidence soaring. Regardless of our age, it's important to still accentuate our best assets and celebrate our femininity. For ladies in their 40's and beyond, control top black translucent tights are an excellent option for covering leg imperfections or belly bulge.

When you place more value on yourself, others will notice and treat you with more respect. Unfortunately, Julie's date ended up being a dud, but she did get compliments on her fabulous dress from both her date and the hostess. Even if you don't have a date, slip into a dress and run some errands. Take note of any difference in the way people interact with you in comparison to when you wear your sweats.

If You Want an Alternative to a Dress, Here are Some More Classy Yet Sassy Options:

Tops:
- Metallics, sequins, and v-neck blouses in complementary colors.
- A fun jacket, like a blazer with sequin trim.

Bottoms:
- Pencil skirts.
- Jeans.

Shoes:
- High heels that expose your pedicured toes.

> "Thank you so much for helping me with this transformation! I now have a sophisticated and attractive look, at least outside of the classroom! Thank you for giving me the confidence to wear sexy dresses that I never thought I could wear!"
>
> —Joy Y., client

Movies

It's that time to go see a funny or romantic movie. What better way to show off another fashionable side of yourself? Movie theaters can easily be ice boxes, so dress for the winter.

Rayne wore a short leopard dress to a movie theater once and vowed never to do it again. "Not to be raunchy, but it was so cold that my nipples were sore. I kept rubbing them like a hobo would do over a fire to get warm. My date must have thought that I had a bad case of fleas. It wasn't easy to concentrate on a three hour movie. When we left, I also noticed that the impressions of the seat covers were on the back of my legs. It looked as if I had cellulite from my thighs all the way down to my knees. Moral of the story: avoid wearing a dress to a movie theater."

It's dark inside a theatre and a fabulous dress is supposed to be seen! Instead of dress, choose something casual, yet alluring. This checklist will come in handy.

Tops:
  * V-neck blouses/sweaters.
  * Jacket.

Bottoms:
  * Jeans.
  * Maxi skirt.

Shoes:
  * High heeled boots.

Ultimate Guide to Style: From Drab to Fab!

Trashy to Classy

How many of you ladies believe **"If you've got it, you might as well flaunt it"?** This frame of mind can send the wrong message and you may find yourself dating a list of men only interested in one thing... a trophy wife, one-night stand, or a booty call. If you want to attract quality men, avoid wearing anything too revealing. On the other hand, if you're only out for a good time and you don't care if the person is only interested in your body that is a different story. During an episode of *What Not to Wear,* a full figured woman insisted on wearing very short and revealing dresses that nearly showed her nipples and private parts. On the episode, six men entered a room and were asked to choose the sexiest photo of the woman. The photos were lined up from the most to the least revealing outfit. The result was unanimous. All six men chose the second to last and last picture. Overall, they agreed that they would prefer to take out a lady who accentuates her assets in a classy, less revealing way.

A mysterious woman is better than one who throws it all in a man's face right away. Let your date imagine what you look like nude. Don't give it away. Dress yourself as an elegantly wrapped gift. That way you can slowly be unwrapped like the precious gift you are. This study really changed the women's outlook. She wanted to grab a dapper business man, but because of her attire she was being viewed as trashy and cheap, even though she was a total sweetheart.

A general rule of thumb when it comes to "dressing sexy and classy" is to pick one area to flaunt and only one. If you want to show off your legs, then don't show too much cleavage. If you want to flaunt a little cleavage, stay away from a very short skirt. Wear something that goes down to at least the knee or right above the knee. Picking more than one area to flaunt will be too much and you will look like an easy target. Same idea goes for nighttime make-up. If you accentuate your eyes with smoky eye shadow and eye liner, go lighter on the lips and cheeks. If you do red or berry lips, then only apply mascara and a natural eye shadow with a little blush. You don't want to overdo it.

As fun and exciting as dating can be, have an idea of where you're going so you can plan your wardrobe accordingly. Men don't have to worry as much, since their choices are slim compared to ours. Ask these questions before you start getting ready for a date:

* Am I going to be standing or sitting?
* Is the party/barbecue indoors or outdoors?
* Is the venue/event formal or casual?
* Will the location be air conditioned?

By answering these questions you can save your feet from aching the next day. In addition, you will not feel the embarrassment of being overdressed at a barbecue or underdressed at a formal occasion. Finally, you will keep your bones from chilling and your armpits from sweating. When you make fashionably educated choices you will be stylin' in chicness, comfort, and confidence!

CHAPTER 6

Hourly Hang-ups: Wear This, Not That to the Office and Why

With today's rough and tough economy, it's even more important to pay extra special attention to your appearance. We know this sounds crazy, but most of us spend a third of our lives at work. Uh, that is a lot of time, ladies. Many of us see our co-workers more than we see our own families. Pretty sad, but completely true, so why not spend that third of your life dressed appropriately? Why not leave a fashionable footprint wherever you go?

Here is a fun little fact: In the work force, your hair and face are the first things that employers and clients notice. We stressed the importance of your hair in the previous chapters. Few people will want to do business with someone who looks grungy, sloppy, and unkempt. The bottom line, it's just not professional. Don't let a bad haircut and outdated appearance cost you the job, deal, or promotion. This applies to you too, entrepreneurs!

Our Stories as Models

"From the start, I would meet with many of the top designers of lingerie companies and, considering that they only were hiring me for my body shape and opinion, I really did not put much effort into my appearance. Looking back, I'm ashamed to say that I showed up wearing my cut off sweatpants, a sports bra, t-shirt, tennis shoes, no make-up, and my hair in a messy bun. I figured since I made everyone laugh and smile, that was enough.

One day Hidi Lee, an established lingerie designer and author, had a life changing discussion with me. Whenever I saw her, she was dressed so stylishly. I could not help but comment on her Dior boots or her fishnet stockings. I would say, "Hidi, you're always dressed so fashionably. Doesn't that get exhausting?" Hidi replied, "Rayne, I'm a designer, so I must dress as a designer. If you're a model, you should look like a model." I glanced down at my worn-out gym shoes and sheepishly smiled and said, "You mean to tell me that I shouldn't show up wearing these worn-out sweatpants and no make-up to cover up my zits?" Hidi laughed and said "Yes."

After my epiphany, slowly, but surely, I started to dress the way I wanted people to perceive me and the way I wanted to showcase myself: as a successful fit model who worked very hard to keep her exact measurements, so she could continue to help pave the way for the perfect bra for all her fellow sized DD women. I want to take a moment now to thank Hidi Lee personally: "Thanks girl!"

From that day forward, I started to dress like a model. I started showing up to the fittings "dressed the part". My clients noticed and started giving me compliments on my fun sense of style. It made me feel great. After all, who doesn't smile more when they get compliments all day long?

With my new outlook on dressing the part, I asked my fit modeling agent, Natasha Duswalt, to ask for a raise for my services. She asked and I started to make more money. I felt like I was worth more and I began making more. Walking the streets of Los Angeles in fashionable attire was way more fun than strutting around in baggy gym clothes!" —*Rayne*

"I was in a very similar position as Rayne, only I was auditioning for lifestyle and commercial print jobs. I spent a lot of time aimlessly driving around Los Angeles to castings and spending useless amounts of energy searching for something to wear for every audition. Most casting agents don't use their imaginations, so it's the job of the model/actress to represent the look that is being cast. Having the basic core wardrobe pieces and knowing which colors bring out your best features is crucial when everyone else at the audition looks just like you!" —*Nicole*

Could you be representing yourself more accurately in your current job position? Let's read on to see what it takes to make a great impression at the interview.

Interviewing For the Job

Have you found yourself in the job market again? If so, you will want to pay extra special attention to your wardrobe while going through

the interview process. No matter whom you are interviewing for ...
DRESS TO IMPRESS!

"For example, in addition to fit modeling, I was also a receptionist during college. When my boss was hiring, I would greet and sign in all the potential employees. The sight of so many people who came in looking disheveled and completely out-of-date was mind boggling. These people were interviewing for a job with wrinkled and faded shirts, white workout gym socks with dress slacks, and hair that had not been styled since Debbie Gibson hit the Top 10 in Billboard. Men have it a little easier: slacks and a dress shirt or a suit with black polished shoes will suffice. Yet, they even screw that up!

However, as women, we have so many options: skirts, slacks, blazers, hair up, hair down, sweaters, button-ups, cardigans and the list goes on and on. If your wardrobe and overall look isn't up to date, the first impression you make is that your skills aren't up to date. The women who came in dressed the worst, I never saw again. I wanted to stop them on their way out, hug them, and exclaim, "I CAN HELP YOU!"—*Rayne*

Here is an interesting fact for you. According to the Bureau of Labor Statistics, retail sales are the highest area of employment: 4,209,500 people, or 3.2 percent of the total American workforce. Other jobs that are in the top 25% of the work force are cashiers, office clerks, counter attendants, nurses, waiters and waitresses, secretaries, general managers, and elementary school teachers. If you're employed or interviewing for one of these positions, you're face to face and greeting people every working day. You're the person who represents the company. We think that is pretty fantastic! Along with a positive attitude and great customer service skills, your appearance is SO important in acquiring one of these positions.

What to Wear to an Interview

When we had our color analysis training, the color expert, Audessa, showed us two pictures: one picture with a woman in a skirt and a blouse and another picture with a woman in slacks and a cardigan. They both looked nice and professional. She asked us, "Which one of these two women do you think makes the most money?" We picked the woman with the skirt. We were correct and 95% of the time, people would choose the woman wearing the pencil skirt. What's our point? Keep reading.

How can you make yourself stand out in the interviewer's mind after he or she sees six other possible candidates for the job? Instead of wearing suits in black and gray, make a lasting impression with other deep colors that look great on you. A beautiful skirt suit, with a fabulous colored blouse is an excellent choice. If you're going to an interview for a corporate position with nothing to wear but a pant suit, make sure you choose one that is up to date and represents you, shows off your confidence, and your ability to go beyond the basics. A great bag, colorful scarf, or some patterned pumps is a great way to add some pizzazz to a neutral suit. You don't want to look generic.

Always add a touch of you. "I recall an interview for an intern position that I had back in my college days. I was only 21 years old at the time and I really wanted to "look professional." I decided to borrow my friend's cheap black suit. I paired it with black flats and a black shirt... BORING! Not one thing I wore that day represented me, except my underwear and no one was going to see that. I did get the internship, but it was unpaid and for college credit. I think you get the point. It must have been my smile and personality, because it sure wasn't the suit that did not fit." —*Rayne*

You're TOO Comfortable at Your Job

If you're an employee who does a great job, at some point, you will desire a promotion. You may not put much thought into your wardrobe; after all, you think, they already love you. Avoid falling into this clothing rut, or you may miss out on greater opportunities, because you're not considering your wardrobe to be a success factor.

What boss doesn't want to have a polished and upbeat employee? Even if you have a standard uniform, we recommend neat and styled hair, a great watch, jewelry (if allowed), comfortable stylish shoes, and a great smile. If you dress nicely, give off a positive vibe, and make the company look great, then you're more likely to keep your job and get promotions. This also works in your favor for any hours that you want to switch or for that day you want to take off. A boss will more likely appease you and go the extra mile to make sure you're a happy employee, if you show you care.

We also suggest learning new things and keeping up with

"I make sure to bring a basic make-up kit along with a washcloth, cleanser and moisturizer. If I need to go from work to an evening meeting, I can stop and refresh my make-up at any restroom. Keeping the basics; foundation, powder, blush, mascara and lipstick and a smoky eye shadow can take my look from day to evening in about 5 minutes."

—*Natasha Duswalt, friend, author, and President of Peak Models & Talent* the latest trends in whatever field you're in. Yes, we know we are not life coaches, but we want you to look better and feel better than you ever thought you could. After all, learning makes you feel good! If we hadn't followed these steps, we most likely would not be running a company today, which brings us to your wardrobe when you're the boss.

Here are three great examples of outfits for business. For a more corporate look, make sure to wear a matching blazer. Caution: wear a tie at your own discretion.

You're the Boss

For those of you who are executives, entrepreneurs, real estate agents, professional speakers, etc., focus on setting a polished "composed" appearance for your employees and clients. If your wardrobe is outdated or disheveled, most likely it will trickle down to your employees and give a bad impression to your clients. Please don't let your business suffer and set a good example.

Chances are you may be public speaking and/or giving business presentations. Here are some pointers on what not to wear in certain circumstances that you may find yourselves in, whether it be for a speech, seminar, television, or a meeting. You want your audience to pay attention to your message, rather than your wardrobe. In our opinion, if your clothes are outdated then your skills and whatever services you are offering may also appear to be outdated.

If you're on the stage wearing a dress that looks like it was made from a Thanksgiving tablecloth or granny panties that are showing VPL's (visible panty lines) through your too-tight pants, you are distracting us from hearing your message. You are also killing the sale. Yes, we have sat through a few seminars cringing at the sight of these things while the presenter's intention was to sell us on joining their program to become a marketing genius. We couldn't get past the distracting unflattering image and figured that we may be better equipped to offer our services to them on how to become a better self-promoter. Everyone can't be good at everything, so we mean all of this in the nicest possible way.

> "I wore one of my new dresses to my council meeting and I fit right in and felt great! You guys are wonderful!"
>
> —Zoe G., client

For those of you who aren't business owners, you can still take ALL these principles and apply them to any job, whether you're a receptionist, customer service representative, or a cashier at Target.

What NOT to Wear on Stage for Speeches:

* Skirt length for women is important, especially on a high stage: the higher the stage, the higher the view up your skirt. Avoid short skirts.

* You don't want to blend in with the background or curtain. Bring an extra outfit, in case you're wearing the same color as the background. Most backgrounds are black or a dark color.

* Avoid VPL's. They are distracting.

* If you wear stilettos and there are cracks in the risers, your heels can get caught or poke through them. Go for a sturdy heel rather than small and pointy.

What NOT to Wear on Stage and Television While Filming:

* Avoid red, white, and black. Cameras don't handle these colors well.

* Compact patterns, such as tiny polka dots or small stripes can create an optical illusion effect, which isn't good.

* Avoid jangly jewelry, as it will be a distraction.

* If you wear glasses, make sure they are non-glare. We want to see your eyes, not the light reflection.

* Silk, gray, and pastels will show and enhance any perspiration caused by nervousness or heat from stage lights. Instead, use polyester blends, rayon blends, cashmere, and merino (light-weight wool). These materials will absorb and hide wetness. Otherwise, wear a nice fitting blazer to keep you looking refined and sweat-free.

What NOT to Wear to the Office and Meetings:

* 5 inch heels.

* Dull looking and out-of-date suits.

* High water pants.

* Too much perfume. (I have made this mistake more than once, but I can't help it and I'm not going to fire myself! —*Rayne*)

* Too much or no make-up (avoid heavy eyeliner and lipstick that is too dark).

* Faded clothing.

* Straggly hair, you need a HAIRSTYLE.

* Sexy dresses and short skirts.

* Scuffed or worn-out shoes.

* Flip flops.

* Anything glittery (make-up included).

* Anything dirty, stained, holey, or wrinkly.

* Spaghetti straps or tube tops.

* Too tight pants (NO CAMELTOES).

* T-shirts with too much information on them:
  ICE CREAM LOVER, I LOVE ITALIANS,
  WEEKEND WHORE, ETC.

Happy Hour

After a long list of what not to wear at work, we finally make it to happy hour. I'm sure that the impromptu invitation to happy hour or dinner has happened to you on more than one occasion. If you're not prepared, most likely you will decline and we wouldn't want you to miss out on fabulous dinners and meeting wonderful new people. Networking is very important!

Here is a great example on how to carry work attire over into the night time. To play down a dress, pair it with a long sweater and boots during the day. After work get into the car, take off your sweater and switch out your boots for high heels. Trade your work bag for a clutch purse. We often keep heels and fold-a-flats in our cars. You just never know when they may be needed. Be prepared for wherever the day may take you!

CHAPTER 7

Baby Talk: Fashion Tips for the Expectant and New Moms

Ahh…the wonders of what will lie ahead when you find out that you're expecting a baby! It's a whole new chapter in your life defined with many emotions, challenges, and changes that you can only understand when you experience this precious gift for yourself. Since Rayne isn't

"I love to pull on my mommy's necklace. It tastes good too!"
—*Chloe Bahia Drake*

a mom yet, I am going to take the lead on this chapter. Brain fog and forgetfulness will creep into the expectant stage and in most cases, last for some time after giving birth. I still have it and my daughter is seven months old as I'm writing this chapter. I'm sure the lack of sleep has something to do with it. I get so frustrated at times, as I rarely ever forgot anything prior to pregnancy. If you also find yourself with a case of "mommy head," go easy on yourself. Bringing in a beautiful new bundle of joy will change you forever. From that day forward, your life will never be the same.

Looking stylish throughout the stages of pregnancy and thereafter can be the furthest thing from your mind. However, if I did it, you can do it. Following these tips will make it easier for you to keep up your appearance, your spirits... and your sanity.

Make the Most of Your Pregnancy Glow

1. Most women look even more stunning due to the pregnancy glow that accompanies a growing belly. Of course you may not always feel your best, so that is when a little make-up (even if it's just lip gloss and mascara) can help turn that frown upside down. You will look better and feel better if you make an effort to keep yourself neat and well groomed.

2. You will get to a point where you will not be able to see your feet, but most likely you will be wearing open toed shoes if you have swelling due to water retention. Keep those feet pretty with a pedicure, because everyone else will see them.

3. A belly band is an ideal accessory. It's great for all stages of pregnancy, especially in the first or second trimester when it's hard to tell if you're pregnant or if you just finished a holiday feast. The band is perfect for covering and layering. Remember, right after giving birth you will have a few extra pounds, so it works then as well.

4. Maternity items that you can dress up or down are the smart way to go. If you're pregnant during a hot summer, maxi-dresses and yoga pants will provide you with the ultimate comfort. If you love jeans, try a stretchy pair made by Sold Design Lab. I wore them until my seventh month and they weren't even maternity pants! H&M has great maternity pants, too. For easy mixing and matching, solid colored items will give you the most options. To change up your outfits use jewelry, scarves or cardigans.

Welcome Your New Wardrobe in Style

Post-Pregnancy Tips:

1. You can wear your maternity and stretchy pants until you fit into your pre-pregnancy clothes. Many women find that their bodies take on a whole new curvaceous shape after the birth of a baby. If this is you, embrace your new body shape and learn how to shop for the right fit. It's a good excuse to go on a shopping spree.

2. When you need a pick-me-up or some alone time, book a facial, mani-pedi, and/or a stylish new hairdo.

3. Once you hit the six month mark, it's time to go through your closet and see what fits and what is worth keeping. We find that our closet clean-out services prove to be transformational in so many ways. It's a way of reinventing yourself and making room for a new improved you!

4. The belly band can be worn to help shrink and tighten your belly back into shape. I wore it a few times a week, even

though it was not comfortable. The combination of the belly band, breastfeeding, and a busy schedule helped me get back into my pre-pregnancy shape.

Five Tips for Nursing Mothers:

1. Dark colors and patterns are great for hiding stains that are inevitable from baby spit up and leaky breast milk.

2. Wearing stretchy cotton, button down shirts, or wrap dresses will give you the most freedom. Button down shirts help keep your back and stomach covered up, so you don't feel so exposed. I was so grateful when I received an especially designed-for-nursing t-shirt from MilkStars. They are comfortable, convenient, and super cute! My favorite is the "Jenny Shirt", designed by our pal, Jenny Beinash!

3. You will often forget which side you nursed on last. I wore a bracelet and switched it back and forth between wrists to remind myself which side to nurse on next.

4. Nursing bras are a crucial investment. Shopping for nursing bras was not fun for me. It was a challenge finding the right size, since my breasts were still changing in size for

> "As a mom of three kids, I don't have a lot of time to get ready. In fact, most days I'm out the door in a pair of jeans and a tee. I like to add a scarf for a bit of color and to feel a little put together. Besides, even if I'm having a "fat day", my scarf will always fit."
>
> —*Stacy Ensweiler, friend and entrepreneur*

the first few months. I eventually bought a few, along with tank tops that open up in the front. You will need easy access to meet the needs of a hungry baby.

5. Nursing covers may come in handy, although I rarely use mine. My daughter doesn't like anything covering her up, as she has to see everything! I have to be discreet and lift my shirt which is another good reason the belly band can be a wise investment.

Accessory Tips:

* Dangling earrings and necklaces will be eye candy for your little bundle of joy, so beware once he/she learns how to grab onto things. I have already lost a pair of my favorite feather earrings. My daughter scrunched them up into an itsy bitsy ball in her tiny little hands. Save those accessories for times when your baby isn't around, unless it's a baby teether necklace, of course. Bracelets and watches will usually be a safe bet.

* A diaper bag will be your new purse. Find one you love. If you want to use a large tote bag, go for it as long as it has a lot of compartments in it. I use my stylish purple Baekgaard oversized tote and I'm very happy with it.

* If you want to get a lot done hands free, I highly recommend a baby carrier. The best part, it increases bonding. I started out using a sling and as my daughter grew bigger, I transferred her into other carriers. My daughter preferred to face outward, so I had a carrier specifically made for that position for awhile until my back could not take it anymore. For hands

free shopping, I also used a custom made designer "fanny pack" like purse.

As challenging as motherhood can be at times, the rewards far outweigh any cons. Nothing beats pure, unconditional love. I absolutely love being a mom. Remember to take care of your needs too. Embrace each stage along the way. Pregnancy is full of excitement and you will experience many clothing size changes. Hang in there. There's a huge light at the end of the tunnel. Post pregnancy can be exhausting, but your baby's innocent eyes staring back at you make all the troubles seem so small.

CHAPTER 8

Age-Defying Attire: How to Maintain Your Style into Your 40's and Beyond!

Congratulations for still putting your best stylish foot forward! Getting older doesn't mean you have to throw on a polyester light blue suit, granny house slippers, and call it a day. Embrace your age and find a stunning new age appropriate look for you. Look classy and be comfortable. No need to be frumpy! After all, 40 is the new 30, 50 is the new 40, and so on.

We will use our client, Carrie, as an example. She is a 49 year old woman who decided to wear a mini zebra skirt and a hot pink shirt to a rock concert. She chose that outfit because it made her feel young. As much as we all want to hold onto our youth, wearing an outfit like that when you're nearly 50 can give off the impression that you're desperately trying to fit in and compete with the 20 year olds. Why not focus on a look that is considered sexy and more alluring for a 50 year old? Sexy at 21 is WAY different than sexy at 50. As women (notice we did not say girls, sluts, or hoochie-mamas, we said WOMEN) we have every right to embrace that lovingly.

Hairstyle

Have you had the same hairstyle for over a decade? If so, it's definitely time for a change. Many women fall into the habit of hanging onto the middle-of-their-back hair days when they were teens. Long stringy hair doesn't equal sexy or youthful. As we age the texture of our hair changes. By no means is it necessary for your hair to go below the middle of your back, unless you're a stripper and need to swoosh it around to your favorite Warrant song, *"She's my Cherry Pie."* Of course, there are exceptions to every rule. Many celebrities have all pulled off their long hair weaves tremendously. Although let's be practical. Most of us don't have $500 to spend on the maintenance for hair extensions every few weeks.

What about your color? Try a few shades darker or lighter for a new look. We suggest consulting with your hair stylist for the right cut, color, and style according to your face shape and skin tone.

Ladies, a bleached mustache is a no-no. We can still see it. We recommend buying a painless facial hair removal tool. We're almost certain you have seen these types of commercials on TV or at your local drugstore's "Seen on TV" section. These are brilliant tools. If you want to take a more aggressive approach, consider laser hair removal. Don't forget about your legs, armpits, and bikini line. Even if you're not dating anyone or your significant other already worships the ground you walk on, keep it smooth and sexy for YOU!

As far as the shape of your eyebrows, they can instantly take years off your face. You will benefit by consulting your esthetician to have the hairs removed by waxing or a method called threading. Threading is a fairly new technique that pulls out the individual hairs with thread without harming your skin like waxing can do. If you have sensitive skin, threading may cause a little irritation. Make sure to test a small area first.

Cleavage and Showing Skin

For all of the fabulous after 40's, you can still show a little cleavage, but avoid showing off your midriff, tummy, butt cheeks, and tramp stamp (tattoo right above your butt). Again, we commend certain celebrities for rocking their rock hard midriff in their 40's, but come on, who has a million dollars to spend on trainers, surgery, chefs, and exercising eight hours a day to pull that off?

The same thing goes for legs. A perfectly fitted pencil skirt ending right above the knee is so sexy. We recommend some black panty hose/tights to wear underneath your skirts to hide those varicose veins that just will not stop "moving in". Spray tans, color enhancing lotion, and make-up for your legs (available at your local drugstore) will help keep your legs smooth and polished. In your 50's and beyond, having a great shape and taking good care of your body is more important and sexier than cleavage and showing skin. Jane Fonda is a SMOKIN' prime example!

Style Personality Pointers

Below we have listed different style personalities and our suggestions for each. Read about <u>all</u> the personalities. Who knows? You might pick up tips that could apply to yourself too.

Creative: When going through your closet ask yourself, "Are these over-the-knee leopard print five inch heels still appropriate for me?" Pay attention to making sure you match your outfits a little more than you did in your 20's and 30's. Perhaps consider trading in that huge red faux fur feather coat for a sleek blazer. You can go wild with shoes, belts, and jewelry, but glam up your mix and match styles with more sophisticated cuts and fabrics.

If you're in your 60's and beyond, keep finding unique pieces to maintain your eclectic look. Don't settle for the "cookie cutter" version of you. However, be careful. You don't want to look like an aging biker, hippie, stripper, or in Rayne's case, a crazy cat lady with all your animal print and patent leather. You can still wear all this, but tone it down...way down. You can still mix and match, but keep the colors in the same family and pick one "eclectic" item to wear per outfit and let it shine...or in Rayne's case, purrrrrr.

Dramatic Fashionista: Don't worry, yes, people are still checking you and your fabulous style out. Wear more color. Buy softer jackets to give you a gentle silhouette. You can still be fashion forward without the studded leather jacket. You can wear big sunglasses to let everyone know, "Yes baby, I still got it!"

If you're in your 50's, you may want to sell all your dresses from your 30's and 40's at a consignment store. Someone else will appreciate them. If you're still sporting or hanging onto your 5 inch high heels, let them go. Your feet will thank you. In your 60's, textured knitted cardigans instead of form fitting jackets will help you make this beautiful transition.

Romantic: Try delicate lace details instead of ruffles. Mix your pastels with darker, sophisticated neutral colors from your color palette. You can stick with delicate patterns, but look for more fitted, sleek sophisticated cuts like a stunning sheath dress. Chiffon and lace will still look smashing on your top half. In your 60's keep the frills and floral for your scarves, bags, undies, and bras. To keep yourself from looking like an outdated prairie girl, add some classic and basic pieces to your wardrobe.

Classically Chic: Make sure your jackets, blazers, and suits are current and updated. To keep your look fresh, add colorful jewelry, scarves, and bags to your sophisticated style. Throw out those basic black Prada shoes you have been wearing and refinishing for the past 10 years. Nothing dates a woman more than square toed shoes. Oh wait, nude pantyhose do. Those of you in your 50's and beyond, add fun layers to your tanks and v-neck shirts in multiple colors (not too bright). Instead of head-to-toe suits, mix and match the jackets and cardigans with other pieces, like jeans and flats for a polished, yet youthful look.

Minimalist: Make sure your jeans are dark and in good condition. We know you love flats, but try a kitten heel. We promise they will not scratch. Update, update, update. Minimalists are known for wearing the same thing too many times. Bring in some romantic influence and pull off a nice billowy blouse with some modern boots and jeans. Then add a few cozy sweaters and camisoles in your favorite colors to your closet.

More Common Sense Tips for Aging Gracefully

* Update your make-up. See a make-up artist at a department store to get your best updated look.

* Use sunscreen on your face and hands religiously.

* Cleanse and exfoliate all your body parts when showering.

* Use organic products (synthetic ingredients break down the elasticity of your skin).

* Eat a healthy balanced diet.

* Drink lots of water.

* Exercise (consult a doctor before starting any exercise program).

* Get a professional mani-pedi; we don't care if they need a saw for your cracked heels. Keep those babies exfoliated!

* We recommend trading in all your painful heels for comfortable ones, like Naturalizer and Sofft Shoes. They both use advanced technology to keep your feet supported and stylish.

What to Avoid:

* Anything too tight.

* Super short skirts (definitely no minis, unless you're Demi Moore).

* Muu muus (these shapeless dresses/tents will age anyone).

* Shapeless sweatshirts.

* Bad hair colored roots.

* Logos or cartoon characters.

* Anything
  from the junior dept.

* Wear less pink, especially
  bubble gum pink. It looks
  like you're trying to be
  a toddler or a junior.
  Try a dusty pink, mauve,
  or magenta instead.

* Glitter
  (make-up or lotion).

* Hair bows. In our opinion,
  if you're no longer in high
  school, please give your
  "Hello Kitty" hair bows to
  your baby sister or little cousins. Embrace being a woman and
  trade in those hot-pink bows for a classy silk scarf.

> "At 47, I was stuck in a rut: t-shirts, tank tops, and too-tight tunics. Fortunately, the go-to gals knew immediately how to tame the T's. Now I'm sporting a more sophisticated and feminine look with soft, free-flowing, romantic blouses. It's amazing how the right clothes can raise one's confidence level to new heights. I'm hanging from the rafters!"
>
> —*Karla Weller, dear friend and client*

"We shall not end this chapter without telling you a story about my grandmother, Minga. She was a die-hard *Creative*. When I was a little girl, I would spend days shopping with her on the streets of New York, digging and bartering for eclectic timeless pieces of "heaven". When she was diagnosed with cancer in her 70's, we were all devastated. In her remaining days, even though she was in a hospital gown with no hair from all the chemotherapy, she rocked a bright blue wig! She made everyone laugh and smile until the day she died. She kept her spirit alive through her blunt comments, smile, and her unforgettable style. She encouraged me to never let ANYBODY or ANYTHING keep me from expressing myself. We want you to shine all the days of your lives!" —*Rayne*

CHAPTER 9

Extracurricular Activities: What to Wear

Working out gets the endorphins going and this is scientifically proven to put you in a better mood, hence making you FEEL better. Why not increase that to FEEL better and LOOK better while you're getting fit?! If you're one of those people who go to the gym wearing any of the following: baggy sweatpants with stains, a big old t-shirt with a cartoon character or an annoying LOGO plastered across it, and/or a scrunchie in your hair, we advise you to think again.

One of our favorite life inspirational writers, Victoria Moran, author of *Creating a Charmed Life* says, "Aside from avoiding anything unflattering (there are usually lots of mirrors in a gym), it's a good idea to stay away from any outfit you don't feel good about. Exercise requires energy, and puttin' on the sweats you wore for three days straight when you broke up with your last boyfriend or girlfriend is an energy-zapper. After all, workout clothes serve both a practical and a psychological purpose. Psychologically, you need special workout gear to convince yourself it's time to work out."

Tops

Look for cuts and shapes that are designed for your body type as you read in Chapter 1. Nike, Adidas, and Stella McCartney are just a few of the companies that offer different fits for women (slim, relaxed, loose, v-neck, tanks) and they still keep you looking fashionable. Dry-fit or moisture wicking material will keep your sweat stains to a minimum. Picking your favorite colors from the darker spectrum of your color palette will keep you looking vibrant and fresh while diminishing the view of sweat marks.

Sport Bras

Sports bras are a must for our busts! Have fun and buy them in your favorite colors.

"Ladies with bigger boobs, I know you may be tempted to just layer a few on, but your girls will not get the support they need and it looks sloppy. Invest in a few sport bras that come in specific bra sizes. For example, instead of buying a large size, buy a fitted size 36DD or whatever your size may be. My favorite one is by New Balance Control Fit Crop. It has so many adjustment capabilities that it gives me the perfect fit. I can even do jumping jacks in them without giving myself a black eye!"—*Rayne*

Bottoms

Cotton is comfortable and your skin can breathe, but it shows sweat marks really badly. "In a spinning class I recently took, the teacher wore an all-cotton gray outfit. When the class was over, she stood up, and was wet everywhere, except for her butt cheeks. A perfect sweat line broke up the two cheeks and from her thighs down she looked like she peed her pants." —*Rayne*

Clothing companies offer great options for all body types. Nike, for example, has a great fitting system for pants. They come in slim, relaxed, and loose in different lengths. "For a sexier vibe, Body Language Sportswear has a Brazilian cut, giving your booty and body a toned look and lift. I am a big fan of this company and the gear has great lasting power." —*Nicole*

For less vigorous workouts, we both like Victoria's Secret online workout yoga pants, not the junior line, PINK, but the section designed for women. You can only find these online. These pants also come in different lengths and cuts and give you many options. Stores like JCPenney are now carrying plus sized options for you.

Choose black pants, since they rarely show any sweat stains and they last longer. Black workout pants often have fun stripes on the side, so pick some colorful ones and add pops of color into your aerobic kicks!

We prefer the relaxed or loose fit on some days and tight cropped pants on other days. If you don't have the body for tight pants yet, go for the relaxed fit. We also prefer the relaxed fit, because sometimes we let our leg hair grow a little longer than we should. With longer pants, no one will know!

These specifically designed pants are durable. Cotton sleeping pants that you may have picked up on sale at a cheap store are dangerous. "One time I was in a Pilates class and a woman had on a pair of cheap cotton pants, which had a huge hole in the crotch. She was not wearing any underwear and her little lady lip was constantly being exposed with every kick and lift she did. I have had one pair of Nike track pants for over six years and they are still in great shape. It's worth buying fitness clothing for working out." —*Rayne*

Underwear

For tight pants/capris, please wear a cotton g-string. Your "you know what," cookie, v-jay jay, hoo ha, will thank you! Polyester and spandex undies are prone to give you yeast infections and vaginitis... not so sexy. Let your "little lady" breathe!

Let's Get Moving!

If belonging to a gym isn't an option for you, we recommend having either a treadmill, stationary bike, or elliptical in your home, preferably facing a TV. Watching your favorite TV shows is a great way to make the time pass faster. A minimum of a half hour a day, 3-5 days a week is a must for heart health. When we really don't feel like working out, we call each other to meet and stroll in our neighborhood. Before you know it, you have chatted, laughed and 30-45 minutes of cardio has gone by! Who knows, you may even meet your future husband, best friend, or next business venture while out and about. Smile in style as you're walking that mile!

For those of you who don't currently exercise, what better time than now to start? One of the most important tips we hear health experts say is "in order to maintain a healthy weight and balanced life you have to make exercising a part of your life...period". Consult your doctor if you are new to exercising. We don't want you to injure yourself. Your body is a beautiful sight to see and explore. Empower yourself by treating your body like a temple. It all starts with you. No matter what size you are, even if you have never exercised in your life, you can do it!

Bathing Beauties: Picking the Right Swimsuit for Your Body Type

No, we did not forget about bathing suits! We know that finding that perfect bathing suit can be a daunting and terrifying task. Keeping a few flattering styles in mind while you shop can help you pick a suit you feel confident wearing. Accentuate your positive assets with bright colors, patterns, and embellishments while you minimize your not-so-hot ones with darker colors and simple styles.

Body Shapes

Pear Shape
One-piece: Plunging neckline or extra flair on the upper section, such as ruffles, funky straps, or other ornamental detailing will keep the attention on the top half of your booty-ful body.

Tops: Try a suit that draws attention to your bust. Go with a print triangle, padded, and/or pattern on top to draw the eye there.

Bottoms: String tied bikini.

Apple Shape

One Piece: Choosing a bold color to show off your curves is our super-HOT first choice. One-piece bathing suits help conceal fleshier stomachs, especially suits with control panels, shirring, or ruching. If you want to add some sex appeal, consider choosing a suit that shows off your back and a low-cut neckline.

Tops: A nice supportive swimsuit for your top half is the key to looking balanced. To cover up your midriff in a two piece, a tankini will do the job. Once you have found a great supportive style, you can rock it and look sexy all day long. If your tummy is hanging over, please go with a slimming one-piece instead.

Bottoms: Boy shorts, high-waisted with a high cut to elongate the leg, and bottoms with embellishments.

Hourglass Shape

One piece: Empire waists or a low-cut bust will flatter the hourglass shape by pulling attention away from the stomach. Remember, you want to feel comfortable and sexy, not exposed.

Tops: For busty hourglasses, try a halter top with under-wire. Choosing a top with a built-in bra for extra support and moderate-to-full coverage will keep your bust in place.

Bottoms: String tied bikini.

Rectangular Shape

One piece: Hello, monokinis and one shoulder suits!

Tops: Women with this shape can get away with wearing many different cuts such as triangle, halter, or bandeau. If you have broad shoulders, go with tops that have thicker shoulder straps.

Bottoms: You can wear most bottoms, including these: low-rise, boy shorts, scoop, and string. If you want to give the illusion of more curves, choose tops and bottoms with embellishments such as ruffles or ruching.

Great one piece suit shapes for every BODY!:

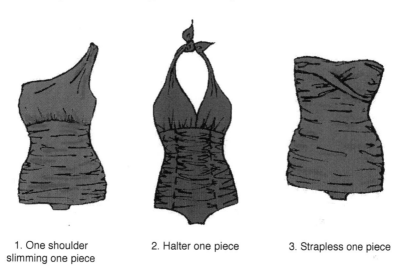

| 1. One shoulder slimming one piece | 2. Halter one piece | 3. Strapless one piece |

Note: Ruching not only works as a great slimmer, but if you are lacking curves, it works as a curve enhancer too.

Petite Pointers:

If you're petite, look for a suit that is high-cut in the leg area. This will make your legs look longer. Avoid boy shorts and skirted bottoms; they make your legs look shorter. Go for a design that runs vertically or stick with bright-colored solids. V-shaped necklines also draw the eye up and down, making you appear taller.

Extra Curvy Pointers:

Many companies are acknowledging that there is a thriving market for full figure swimwear that is flattering and slimming. "I've had the pleasure of working with designers from Swim Systems, Sunsets Inc., and Aerin Rose on the fits of their full busted/full figure swimwear. I have seen the meticulous detail and caring that goes into fitting a voluptuous body. Plus sized women are FIGUREing out there is no need to hide during bathing suit season! Aquatic classes, the beach, and swim parties are for their enjoyment too!" —*Rayne*

The best suit for plus size is a patterned, slimming one piece or swimdress. These suits are designed to make you appear slimmer and accentuate all your positives while diverting the eye away from any parts you may want to hide.

Shop for a Bathing Suit That Has the Following:
* Built-in bra. One that you can buy in standard bra measurements. (Victoria's Secret, Sunsets Inc., Swim Systems, and Aerin Rose are recommended companies that carry swimsuits in bra sizes).

* Supportive underwire.

* Thicker comfortable straps.

* Fully lined, preferably with powernet, for optimizing tummy control.

* Diagonal patterns and ruching.

Sarongs are a nice option when you're outside of the water. They provide extra coverage if you want it and add a little more pizzazz to your swimwear.

Avoid:

* Two toned suits that will cut you in half.
* Horizontal stripes, as they will make you appear wider.
* Too tight suits.

You will be able to find most selections online. Be sure to follow the company's size chart and check on their refund/exchange policy. Sizing swimsuits properly can be tricky. We suggest ordering the same bathing suit in two separate sizes to get the best fit. For example, if you're a 22w try a 22w and 24w. If you're a size 8 in women's clothing, you may want to try a size 10 also. See which one fits better and return the other one.

It's very fashion friendly to wear a solid bottom with a patterned top or a solid top with a patterned bottom. Mixing and matching is fun and makes for more swimsuit combinations. Like body shapes, you may fit into more than one category. Some women are tall and slender; others are petite and pear-shaped. Ask yourself these questions: "How does your behind look in the swimsuit?" "Is it cutting into the flesh of your rear end or sagging?" "Are your breasts lifted and covered or are they floppy and coming out the side?" Knowing the category or categories you fit into will help you narrow down the swimsuits to consider. Spend your summer at the beach instead of inside the dressing room!

Ultimate Guide to Style: From Drab to Fab!

CHAPTER 10

Lights, Camera, Accessories: Purses, Scarves, and Sunglasses...Oh My!

Keeping up with the latest trends can be very time consuming and expensive. Don't fret shopping pets, once you have your basic wardrobe in your closet this becomes a cinch! For example, as we write this book, neon colors are in style. If you can't afford to buy high quality pieces or don't feel comfortable wearing neon, then buy some "trendy" accessories instead, like a neon green bag or bracelets.

Purses

Purses, like shoes, should always be stylish, clean, well made and up to par! A woman's social status is often judged by her purse. A cheaply made bag makes you look just that… cheap. You carry all your make-up, credit cards, and identification, basically everything that symbolizes who you are in your bag. Protect YOU with a powerful purse! A purse that says, "I have been dragged on the floor and plastered with someone else's name," says "I don't know who I am or what I want to represent!" A quality purse says "I deserve to be held in high regard: externally and internally". Avoid buying the knock off/fake versions of your favorite designers. Strive for real…a real you.

We are by no means telling you to go out and spend thousands of dollars or your children's college fund on a Louis Vuitton. In our opinion, if you're going to walk around advertising a name on your clothes or bag, you should be paid for it. However, Louis and Chanel also represent a timeless era of class. If you can afford these luxuries, then go for it. Take good care of them. They are investment pieces.

On the other hand, if you think paying $5,000 for a bag isn't in the market for you, and you would like your purse to represent the successful person

you are, opt for a good leather or faux leather handbag. You can get a great bag from a consignment store, discount store, or you could just order one from eBay. Check eBay for lightly used designer bags from your favorite brands and search for authentic bags with certificates. You can also look in department stores like Macy's for the end of season sales. We recommend T.J. Maxx, Marshalls, and Loehmann's for great quality at a discount price. Almost every bag we have ever owned has been purchased from one of these places.

We suggest "picking out" a purse that matches your height. The right sized purse, like the right sized pattern, can make you look leaner, taller, and more polished. On the other hand, the wrong sized purse can make you look sloppy, out of style, larger, and wider.

For example, Rayne is 5'10", so she picks out larger purses to match her height. Nicole is 5'6", so she uses medium purses. Last, but not least, for those of you who are shorter than 5'5", smaller purses are the way to go.

We also recommend trading in your black or brown purse for a colorful one that is in your color palette or the hottest color of the moment. Steer away from the norm. You don't have to match everything; it adds a unique sense of style. Whether it's a Louis, a Prada, or an unknown beauty made with love and detail, it's the holder of all that is you. A "stylish, classy, perfect size for you" purse shows the world that you and your success can be taken seriously and acknowledged!

Scarves

A colorful scarf adds a polished look to any outfit. Make sure that the scarf complements your skin tone and hair color. Choose a color from your color palette and it will make you look energized and well rested, even if you're not.

Here are Four Simple Ways to Tie a Scarf:

1. **Bow:** A bow is playful, yet oh so classy! Take a long or short scarf and tie a bow around your neck, move it to one side and fluff! This adds a touch of class to any outfit, even a t-shirt and jeans!

1. Bow

2. **The Loop:** For longer scarves, put both ends together, wrap around your neck, take the loose ends and pull them though the loop, then adjust it to where you want it placed.

2. The Loop

3. **Regular Wrap:** Wrap around your neck so each end hangs evenly. This is a perfect way to add a pop of personality to your outfit. Choose a leopard scarf, pair it with a solid colored tank, matching colored jeans, and let your scarf do the talking...in this case, the roaring!

3. Regular Wrap

4. **Infinity:** It's like a scarf, but it's a full circle. No fussing with it. Just double it up around your neck and you're good to go.

4. Infinity

These are the top four neck wraps, but you can also wear the scarf as a headband, bandeau, belt, or wrap. We find the other wrap styles take a little more effort and thought. We like simple, sassy, and sophisticated.

Sunglasses

Think of buying sunglasses as buying an attitude. When you're wearing great quality designer shades, nothing can stop you from feeling like a million bucks. Glance at yourself in a reflection, slide your glasses down to the middle of your nose and say "Are you talking

Ultimate Guide to Style: From Drab to Fab!

to me?" or for those of you who like a little slang, "Dang girl... you be lookin' fly!" I have said both of these lines to my reflection in the mirror while I was wearing my favorite Versace pair. —*Rayne*

Glasses are like handbags. They are timeless investments that can relay many different messages in just one sheer slip on. "Before buying my Versaces, I used to buy sunglasses at Ross and T.J. Maxx, spending anywhere from $20-$30 per pair. I would always break them, scratch the lenses, or lose them at the theater, in dressing rooms, client's homes, and public restrooms. Finally, I decided it was time for me to graduate from "baby cheap sunglasses" to a "quality designer sunglasses" state of mind. As an adult, I figured I should be able to take good care of a pair.

I chose Macy's for my successful sunglasses shopping trip. I spent a half hour finding the perfect ones for me and I was ecstatic when I found them. I walked out of the mall feeling like a hot rock star! I'm not exaggerating. The point being: INVEST. Look for a well-made quality pair with lenses made from scratch-resistant, impact proof polycarbonate. You can feel like a rock star, movie star, or just simply a million bucks with a perfect pair of sunglasses.

NOTE: I have not lost, scratched, or broken my Versaces. Nicole has owned two pairs of Dior sunglasses for five years. Take our word for it: when you make a good investment on something, you take better care of it." —*Rayne*

How to Pick Your Frames

First, observe the shape of your face. An overall tip is to choose a pair that are the opposite shape of your face and proportionate to the size of your features. It's just like choosing a purse or patterns for your wardrobe. For example, if you have a square face with pronounced features choose rounder, softer frames. If you have small features with a diamond shape, try frames with detailing that are oval shaped.

Find Your Face Shape:

Oval: Wider at cheek bones, soft curved jawline.

Heart: Wide forehead, prominent cheekbones, pointed chin.

Diamond: Wider at the cheekbones and narrow equally at the jaw line and forehead.

Rectangle: Longer in length than it is wide, usually square jawline.

Square: Even in length and width, very square jawline and forehead.

Round: Soft jawline and chin, usually full cheeks and narrow forehead.

Oval

Heart

Diamond

Rectangle

Square

Round

Keep in Mind the Following Guidelines
When Shopping for Your Perfectly Shaped Glasses:

Oval: You're in luck, since the majority of styles look good on oval faces. Geometric or rounded frames look best.

Rectangle: Emphasize the width of your face, rather than the length by choosing a taller, curved, or rounded style. Taller frames will shorten the length of your face. Avoid small round frames.

Round: Help sharpen your features with squared, rectangular, or thick frames.

Heart: Round, cat-eye, and aviator styles (frames that are heavier on bottom and flat on top) can add width to the lower face.

Square: Rounded, cat-eyed, and oval shapes soften the shape of your face. Avoid square shaped frames.

Diamond: Try oval frames for a balanced look.

Coloring tip: We love basic colors for glasses: blacks, neutrals, navys, and grays. They are easier to match with outfits!

Style tip: Even though your favorite celebrity is sporting some new over-the-top glasses, it doesn't mean they are right for you. You're unique and beautiful, so stay true to yourself.

Fitting tip: No matter if you're wearing sunglasses or eyeglasses, they should sit nicely on your face. There should be no movement, sloshing, or sliding down your nose when you smile or laugh and your peepers should be looking out of the middle of the lens. We recommend having your glasses fitted, just like we recommend getting a fitting for your boobies.

PS. If anyone knows somebody at Ray-Ban, please let them know that Rayne, would like them to make some glasses for ladies with bigger features. Their glasses look so great on stars like Kate Moss, but ridiculous on me!

Tips for Smaller Scale Women

If you're on the more delicate and dainty side, like Nicole, your facial features are smaller and your bone structure will be on the small to average size.

* Wear smaller patterns; large patterns will swallow you up.

* Wearing clothes of the same color hue will make you look taller.

* Wear delicate accessories.

Tips for Larger Scale Women

If you're large and in charge, like Rayne, your features are more prominent. You have a bigger bone structure and may be taller or more voluptuous than average.

* Wear larger patterns, but not TOO large. Wearing small patterns will make you look bigger in all the wrong places.

* Wear larger jewelry.

* Keep your hair full and wavy.

Shoes

For your shoes, we are open to anything except square-toed pumps, boots, or slip-ons. Oh wait, super pointy-toes are also off our style radar. An almond-toe and peep-toe pump has been in style since the 1950's. Soft pointed kitten heels are a great option if you want to add a touch of elegance. Here is where you can really add some pizzazz to your outfit with "pops" of color and cool prints.

Tip for "plump" ankles; stay away from the straps and purchase similar colors to your skin tone to create a slimming effect.

For boots, if you are petite go for mid-calf or lower. You don't want to be over powered. For everyone else, we love boots in all heights, patterns, and materials.

Here is a recap: For purses, know what size works best with your size and features. Stay away from cheaply made and knock off purses, which are usually stiff and hard to zip. Scarves add a lot of class and sophistication. We love them! They can be used to add a pop of color and add extra style to any outfit. Find a pair of sunglasses that make you look and feel important. Familiarize yourself with your face shape and which shapes look best on you. It never hurts to get a trustworthy friend's opinion. For jewelry, follow the same principles in regards to your size. Accessories are a great way to add your personal touch to any outfit.

CHAPTER 11

Pack It Up, Baby!: How to Pack Smart and Fashionably for Travel

In the past, we were both a little naive on the subject of packing. We always over packed, yet forgot that one "important" thing that we told ourselves we would not forget. Whether it was a bathing suit, contact eye solution, or just plain having packed for the wrong climate, we finally got fed up with packing the wrong clothes. So we started taking down notes and researching what was truly necessary to put into our suitcases.

"As I was writing this chapter, I thought I had the whole packing thing down, only to forget something again! I thought to myself, "Gosh darn it, I should have followed my own tips in this chapter!"

It was the beginning of November and I was on an impromptu trip. I flew to Las Vegas to help out our business mentor, Tom Antion http://www.Antion.com, with a seminar. I packed very lightly. On the last day, I found myself at a five star resort with six pools, three jacuzzis, and no bathing suit. The hotel sold a few in the casino, but none of them fit me, since I have to buy "bra sized" bathing suits and 34DD is "special" a.k.a. mutant sized. What to do? I had to take a cab to Walmart to shop for a bathing suit, since it was my only option at the time. How frustrating!

Of course, when I got to Walmart, there were no tops leftover and all the one pieces were size 16 and above. I ended up buying a bottom from the junior section (which is against my own rules) and a sports bra. I was left with no other choice. Embarrassing. On that day, I made a vow to myself that I would always follow our packing list." —*Rayne*

Fashion Travel Tips

1. **Weather**

   Go to weather.com or Google your destination to what climate to pack for. You don't want to waste precious space in your suitcase by packing heavy winter coats or high heels.

2. **Split Up Your Money, Honey!**

   It's unfortunate that we have to talk about this subject, but tourists are known to get robbed. It's a good idea to split up all your means of paying for things. "For example, once I get settled into the hotel, I keep some cash/credit cards in my luggage, some in my bra (old habit from gambling in Las Vegas), and the rest in my wallet. If some desperate person wants to steal my stylish purse, he or she will not get all my goodies. Definitely split up your passport and driver's license/ID. I often bring an expired ID with me just in case." —*Rayne*

3. **Three-Ounce Rule**

   Three ounces is still the liquid travel maximum. Stores like Target usually have see-through bags that you can buy to hold your shampoos, conditioners, facial wash, etc. If you don't want to go through the hassle of refilling these items, you can purchase your favorites at **http://www.3floz.com/**. This website is completely travel-friendly. You can find your favorite products along with ones that you may have always wanted to try, but hesitated on buying the full bottle.

4. **Wardrobe**

   Pack things that have a multi-purpose or can be transformed from day to night. For example, pack a maxi-dress if you're traveling somewhere tropical. It can be worn during the day as a beach dress or it can be layered with a cute top and heels for nighttime. It can also be worn as a nightgown. Great thinking, right?

   a. Pack clothes in the same color family (blue/red, gray/yellow, turquoise/magenta). With that arrangement, you can mix and match items and still make it look like you have twice as many clothes as you do. Pack something fancy and formal. While traveling, you will most likely meet other travelers. If the opportunity presents itself, be prepared for nice dinners and making new friends.

b. Lay out all the outfits you plan on wearing, including the accessories you will need. Planning ahead this way will keep you from forgetting a belt, a bracelet, or in one recent case, a boot. Keep reading.

5. **Have Your Friend Carry One of Your Outfits**

This may sound crazy, but if you're traveling with your significant other, you should each pack at least one outfit for the other. If one piece of luggage gets lost, you will both still have some outfits until the luggage is found. I know what you're thinking, lost luggage only happens on sitcoms. Uh, if you have ever watched Bravo's Real Housewives series, it happens every season with someone in every cast. Just saying, sh#*t happens to everyone. It may be a pain in the butt, but you will thank us if this happens to you!

6. **Carry-on Luggage**

Packing your carry-on bag efficiently is the most important thing you can do in life! Just kidding, but it's pretty important. Plane flights, like the rest of life, can be unpredictable. You can be sitting on the plane getting ready to take off when all of a sudden the captain comes on to tell everyone that there has been an unexpected weather change. Take off is expected in an hour, yet it could end up being three hours later. You might also get caught flying in a circle for two hours, because the flight plan has been changed or you may even have an overnight delay in Omaha, Nebraska. You will thank your lucky stars that you read this part of our book and followed our instructions. You don't want to be stuck without medications, a contact case and solution, clean underwear, clean t-shirt, fresh socks, deodorant, or worse, a toothbrush. Whenever you need to feel fresh, brush your teeth and change your undies. You will feel like a brand new woman!

a. In addition to your toiletries carry any "must have" wardrobe in your carry on as well. When I was working for the Miami Swim Show, the airline accidently transported one of the models and my luggage to Dallas, Texas. We instantly bonded over this and had quite the first night. We had flown in to Miami from California and arrived at 10 pm and we had to go check into the hotel. Then, take a taxi back to the airport at 1:30 am to get our late arriving luggage. Did I mention we had to wake up at 6:30 am to do five swimsuit runway shows? Yes, we were exhausted. We could've avoided this by having our "must haves" along with us and let the airline deliver the luggage to us the next day. So if you are in a wedding or an event, keep your outfit/bridesmaid dress/performance wear with you. —*Rayne*

7. **Beach Bag (if you're going to the beach)**
When packing for the beach, consider pre-packing whatever you can into a beach bag inside your backpack or suitcase. Especially if you're travelling with kids, this will prove to be a timesaver. You don't want to be driving around town looking for a bottom to your bathing suit or 50 SPF sunblock for the kids. As soon as you get to the hotel you

can reach into your suitcase, grab your beach bag, and head out to the sand. We can already taste the margaritas!

8. **Shoes**

   Use shoe bags or plastic bags for your shoes. These will keep your luggage odor and dirt free.

   a. **Note:** Make sure you pack both shoes. As I was writing this chapter, I was in Canada when I realized that I had packed only one knee-high leopard boot! While packing for the trip, I had been trying on some outfits and pulled out a boot to see if it would match, then forgot to put it back in the suitcase. Pack both of your shoes at once and don't take them out until you get there. —*Rayne*

9. **Stash It**

   As a space saver; you can stash belts, accessories, and socks into your shoes and/or extra clutch.

10. **Roll It**

    Look for fabrics like cotton knits or blends (nylon/lycra/spandex) that easily roll up. These will come out wrinkle-free and they pack better.

11. **Technical Stuff**

    Double check to make sure you have everything you will need to charge your technical devices.

12. **Tell Someone You Trust the Details of Your Trip**

    This has nothing to do with fashion and may seem juvenile, but it's necessary. Tell a family member or loved one where you're going, with whom, and any other detailed information.

We have watched enough Dateline and FBI Files to know that this is a very important tip. On these shows, people go missing and it always saves time or YOUR LIFE if someone knows where you're supposed to be. Better safe than sorry, should anything happen to you.

Packing for Fashion

Have you ever received a last minute call from a friend asking you to be ready within the hour? How exciting! You're taking a spontaneous weekend trip. In this scenario, don't panic. Just as you would with extended vacations, pack things that have dual purposes. When you have a list, you can rest all the way to your destination in a stress free fashion. Follow this list and have a blast!

Packing Options for a Sunny Weather:

* ★ Maxi-dress and/or comfortable cotton skirt.

* ★ Sundress.

* ★ Shorts.

* ★ Tank top and loose flowing blouse.

* ★ Bathing suit.

* ★ Sun hat.

* ★ T-strap sandals or fancy flip flops.

* ★ Heels, wedges, or peep-toe flats that show your toesies.

* ★ Earrings (hoops, feathers, chandeliers).

* ★ Clutch.

* ★ Pajamas, if you don't sleep naked.

* Minimum of three pairs of undies (you can never have enough clean ones).
* Foldable beach bag.
* Sunglasses.
* Sunblock.
* Toiletries.

Packing Options for a Cold Weather:
* Warm cozy jacket.
* Comfy sweaters.
* Dark jeans.
* Flat and comfortable boots.
* Long sleeve cotton shirt for layering.
* Leggings.
* Cami/tank top for layering.
* Thick socks.
* Scarf.
* Studded earrings (ones that will not get caught on your scarf).
* Long necklaces.
* Clutch.
* Pajamas.
* Bathing suit.
* Toiletries.

"Until a recent stay at a surprisingly disgusting hotel, I never bothered packing pajamas. However, all the other hotels were booked and

Ultimate Guide to Style: From Drab to Fab!

I was stuck in a dingy, dirty hotel. I didn't want to sleep naked and expose my skin to whatever may have decided to crawl all over me. I had to go to the only store that was open; Walmart, again." —*Rayne*

Planes, Trains, and Automobiles; Chic and Comfortable

No matter where you're going or how you're getting there, here is what we suggest you travel wear:

* **Maxi Dress:** We love wearing maxi dresses when traveling, because they feel like nightgowns, yet they look feminine and well put together.

* **Cotton T-Shirt With your Jeans:** Shirts with polyester, lycra, etc. can get a little stinky in the armpit area after a few hours, even with deodorant. With dark denim, if you sit or spill anything on yourself, it will not show up.

* **Earrings:** As long as they are comfortable and not too heavy. "Be careful not to lose them when you fall asleep on the plane. I've lost a few great pairs that way. Lesson learned. Now I take them out before I snooze!" —*Nicole*

* **Flat Mid-Calf Length Boot or Shorter:** Cover up your footsies, even if you're going to a vacation on the beach. Traveling can be hazardous to your feet. They can get stepped on by the late arriving passengers running through the airport. Also, temperatures can change from hot to freezing cold. Lightweight slip-ons are also great for traveling.

* **Chic Jacket:** For colder climates wear leather/faux leather and for warmer climates wear a jean jacket.

* **Scarf:** Can double as a pillow and blanket. Choose a lightweight one for warmer climates and a heavier one

for cooler climates. Hallelujah to fashion that acts as your comfort haven!

* **Watch:** Will come in handy, as you don't want to keep digging through your purse for your phone to check for the time, so you can be on time. It also adds a little pizzazz to every outfit.

* **Travel Pillow:** My travel pillow is in the shape of a cat. I love sleeping on it on the airplane! —*Rayne*

These suggestions will help you prepare for a successful, safe, and fashionable trip. The more you plan ahead, the less you will worry. You don't need to look like a big sloppy mess, a disheveled mom on the run, or a gym rat on vacation. Why not be sexy, confident, and true to your personality all the days of your life? We hope you enjoy your next trip!

CHAPTER 12

Out With the Old; In With the New!: The Closet Clean-Out Process

Easy as 1, 2, 3!

If you're like most people, you open your closet door, look at a bunch of clothes, and feel like you have nothing to wear. Don't worry! You don't have to throw out your over-the-top wedding dress you wore at your third wedding or the 40 Hawaiian shirts you will need for the next luau-themed office party. We will help you remove the things that are unflattering, outdated, worn or torn, or stained. This process will help free up space for a new and improved you! Following the closet clean-out, we will have you create a list of what can be purchased to complete your new future looks in the next chapter.

Step 1: Make Three Piles:

* **Keep Pile:** Consists only of things that fit you, flatter you, and those things that are fashionable. All sentimental items can be stored in a box or treasure chest.

   When making the 'keep' pile, ask yourself the following questions:
   1. Have you worn this garment in the past year?
   2. Does the garment have any stains, tears, or pilling?
   3. Does this item fit you properly?
   4. Is the fabric comfortable?
   5. Is the fabric in good shape?
   6. Does the cut flatter your body type?
   7. Is this your style personality?
   8. Does the color look good with your skin tone, hair color, and/or eye color?

* Tailor/Repair pile: Items that look great on you, but may need a little mending or tailoring. An item such as a jacket that can be updated by switching out the buttons or shortening its length would fit into this category.

* Donate pile: Clothes that don't fit, have not been worn in more than a year, faded or torn clothing, and colors that don't flatter you.

Step 2: Be Proactive:

1. Take your repair pile to the tailor sooner than later.

2. Sell any designer items at a consignment store, on eBay, or **PoshMark.com**. A second-hand consignment store will usually offer you 30% to 40% of what they will be selling it for. For the most part, they only take stylish items that are in need for a specific season. Personally, we find selling clothes on eBay is time consuming, but it's definitely a lucrative option.

3. Have a "clothing swap" party with your friends. Tell all your friends to bring over their unwanted items and swap. We recommend "swapping" over cocktails. It's so much fun!

4. Donate them to Goodwill or Salvation Army.

Selling Tip: "I went to sell my unwanted clothing at a consignment shop. When the buyer was examining the clothes, a pair of my dirty underwear flew out and went behind the counter! The buyer had to pick them up and hand them back to me. How embarrassing. Did I mention they were my "I ran three miles and sweated like a piggy" gym underwear? Be sure to double check the bags and pockets you take to the consignment shops. You don't want this to happen to you!" —*Rayne*

Step 3: Organize Your Closet

Follow These Tips:

* NO MORE WIRE HANGERS! Recycle them. They are dirty, snag your clothes, and most importantly, they are not good for the environment. Most dry cleaners will take your old hangers. Replace them with plastic or wooden hangers.

Also, purchase a few multi-purpose ones for skirts and slacks. This saves a lot of space. You can score big with the closet organizing items at Ross, Marshalls, and T.J. Maxx.

* Take your clothes out of the plastic dry cleaning bags. Due to the chemicals, the bags can be toxic for your wardrobe and for you.

* Coordinate your clothing. Sort by the type of garment and then by color. For example, make a section for your button down shirts and organize them by color starting with black or darker colors and ending with white. If you prefer, you can break the shirts down even further into sleeve lengths. Continue to organize your shirts, pants, skirts, and dresses in a similar fashion. For your t-shirts, sweaters, and jeans, make tidy stacks and place them on shelves or in a dresser drawer.

"Rayne and Nicole are amazing. When I first met them, I was so stressed. They calmed me down and helped me to see myself through their eyes. I look a lot better that way! They came to my house and gently, but firmly told me which items had to go. Then we shopped for replacements and now it's a LOT easier to get dressed and feel confident. I've worked with them again and again and I always recommend them because they're AWESOME!"

—Harmony J., client

Ultimate Guide to Style: From Drab to Fab!

* If you have a smaller closet, organize according to the season. Anything out of season can be stored in garment bags tucked under your bed or in a storage space.

* For shoes, be creative; just get them off the floor. You can take photos of them and paste the pictures to the inside of clear boxes, a hanging shoe bag over the door, or a shoe rack.

A friendly note: After a successful closet clean-out, you may feel a bit lost. Don't worry, it's a normal feeling after removing clutter. You're in the process of transforming into a more polished you.

Step 4: Make an Assessment List of What You Need

It's time to assess what items you will need in creating an easy to wear and pair wardrobe. Before you buy anything, our job is to help you build your core wardrobe. This is the key to dressing without the hassle or any second guessing.

Your CORE wardrobe is made up of these basic pieces:
* Blazer.
* Slacks.
* Pencil or A-line skirt.
* Dark wash jeans.
* Blouse.
* Cashmere sweater.
* Leather, faux leather, and/or a jean jacket.

These are called 'investment pieces". For example, a great pair of quality slacks may cost you $275. However, you will wear them for five plus years, making your investment merely pennies every time you slip into them. Your CORE wardrobe will not go out of style for years. Spend the extra money and get them tailored if needed. You can buy a $13 blouse, pair it with your "perfect-for-you" pants, add some trendy jewelry, and look like a million bucks. Since your core wardrobe is top notch, everything else will LOOK top notch.

CHAPTER 13

Make a List and Check it Twice: A Shopping Plan of Attack

Shopping is truly an art form that we have mastered and so can you! Many people make a list when they grocery shop, check it twice, and may even cut out coupons to save some extra money, yet somehow they fail to apply the same principles to shopping for a wardrobe. We want you to make the comparison. After you have gone through your closet, all you will have left are amazingly exquisite and "unexpired" items that will keeping you looking fab. Are you ready for the list?

The List

Suits:

Dark pantsuit in a color that flatters your skin tone.

Soft neutral-colored suit.

Tops:

3 button-up shirts.

3 blouses.

2 fun tops/t-shirts.

6 sweaters; 3 neutral, 3 colored.

Jackets:

Leather, faux leather, and/or jean.

2 Blazers (can be taken from the suits listed above).

Three-quarter length wool coat (for those of you with winter weather).

Bottoms:

3 pairs of slacks (can be taken from suits listed above).

3 skirts of different lengths and styles, which will be determined by what looks best for your body type.

3 pairs of jeans of different lengths so that they can be worn with flat shoes or high heeled shoes, and at least one pair of dark wash.

Dresses:

2 solid colored dresses.

1 patterned dress.

Shoes:

Black heels.

Colored heels.

Print patterned heels.

Black and neutral
colored boots.

Black and neutral
colored flats.

Accessories:

Handbag or clutch.

Belts that give you a sexy waistline.

Scarves and jewelry. Try a trendy store, like Forever 21,
for stylish accessories at a great price.

Wristwatch.

Even if you can't purchase everything on this list all at once, print it out and check it off as you acquire the items. Starting with your **CORE** wardrobe is recommended. Choosing at least one item from each section will give you the freedom to start putting outfits together. For example, buy one great pair of jeans to go with a colorful blouse, rather than buying everything from the bottoms section of the list all at the same time. This method will help you stay on track and keep you from purchasing clothes that you don't need.

Mixing and matching according to the season will be a cinch once you have everything on your list. Tossing out your dull worn-out blouses and replacing them with this season's hottest "pop of color" trend will give you a nice boost of confidence. Remember to factor in your age and profession when shopping. For example, a college woman in her 20's would do best with four pairs of denim and two pairs of slacks. In contrast, an up and coming film executive may find that an additional pair of slacks (making four pairs), instead of three, would prove to be more practical.

"As far as shoes go, most women will agree that you can never own enough. I'm a big fan of colorful and crazy print shoes since they add pizzazz to almost any outfit. Even if you choose to dress more conservatively, you can let your feet steal the show with your own unique personality. Of course, I recommend leopard print heels in any color. If you're not a leopard print kind of gal, go for a bold colored stiletto!" —*Rayne*

Now that you have your list you may be wondering how to shop for the right fit. There's no settling when it comes this. Another thing to consider when shopping is that different designers, brands and stores don't size their clothing the same. It's okay to go up or down a size. Even though your measurements are the same, you may find that the size you buy can fluctuate within at least four sizes. For example, if you usually wear a size 8, you may find that you can also wear a 6 or 10 depending on the brand. If it looks great and you can breathe in it, go with it.

What to Look for When Picking Out Items With a Great Fit:

Shirts:
* You want to have room to move, so allow for some movement across the shoulder area. Swing your arms back and forth to make sure the shirt isn't restrictive.

"Be careful not to tear a hole in it. It has happened to me. Not so sexy!" —*Nicole*

* Save the peep holes for the bedroom, otherwise known as the gaps between buttons in the bust area. Check for these in your button ups and cardigans. Go up a size and have it taken in on the sides, if necessary.

Sleeves:

* Long sleeves that finish at your wrist bone.

Jackets:

* Look for a jacket that will fasten easily. If you can't zip or button up easily, go up a size.

* Longer jackets and trench coats (not blazers) look best when they are slightly longer than your skirts or dresses.

* Allow for extra room in your winter coats so if you decide to wear multiple layers or bulky sweaters, everything will still fit nicely.

Skirts:

* Skirts that end at the skinniest part of your leg, such as below the knee or right above.

* Midi-skirts that end at the skinniest part of your calf.

* For easy breathing, make sure you can sit down easily and get a few fingers inside your waistband. Walk into every meeting and sit with confidence and ease!

Pants:

* For pants that are whiskering, showing love handles, or creating the dreaded camel toe, try the next size up.

* Wide leg, flare, and straight pants that just skim the floor in the back and cover the foot in the front. Pants that are too long will collect dirt in the back and the hem of the pants will start to shred. This isn't a good look for anyone.

* If you have to lie down on the floor and suck in your stomach or ask for a pair of pliers to zip them up, give yourself a big hug and get a bigger size. When you're comfortable, you will smile a lot more!

Shopping Tips

1. When you find your favorite clothing brand, the one with a perfect fit, stick with that brand. We love major department stores for this purpose. They keep up to date with all the brands they carry and you can always count on them to have sales and discounts. Whatever you do, don't buy something just because it's on sale. Only buy it if it's on your list!

2. Bring a trustworthy friend along with you. Salespersons may prompt you to buy everything in order to make a higher commission and/or they are nice and don't want to hurt your feelings. Have you ever found yourself taking the salesperson's advice and then get home and think, "I look incredibly silly wearing this hot pink trapeze dress? Nicole and Rayn would totally slap me on the back of my hand if they knew I bought this!" Go with your gut instincts and with any suggestions that ring true for you after reading

this book. You will be making smarter decisions for yourself in no time.

3. For basics, like suits, slacks, and pencil skirts, choose classic clean pieces with minimal extras, such as buttons, ruffles, pleats, patterns, etc.

4. Choose colors that look flattering on you. Refer back to Chapter 3.

5. Is it a quality, long lasting piece that you will not have to replace next year?

6. If you don't LOVE it, leave it at the store.

7. You would be wise to leave the tags on until you wear it. That way if it sits in your closet or you happen to find a similar item that tickles your fancy even more, you can still return it.

Get ready to see a world of difference in your everyday life once you really take the initiative to shop according to your body type and color palette. Most importantly, remember to stay true to your personality. Every woman has a "cat-walker" in them. Find that little girl inside of you that used to play dress up and go get 'em girls!

WARNING, LADIES: Shopping can get very exhausting. Wear clothes that you can easily slip on and off, shoes included. Prepare ahead of time by eating something and bring along some snacks. You will need the energy. When we shop, we always take something to drink, a bag of trail mix, and/or an energy bar.

Sales Racks and Discount Chain Tips

For the thrifty shoppers, we recommend getting your list handy and heading straight for the sales racks. You will find the best deals there. Most likely the racks will be a complete disaster and you may find yourself overwhelmed, but don't give up. The short term hard work will contribute to a long term payoff: the perfect wardrobe at a better price!

Once you learn what to look for and what looks great on you, it will become much easier. When shopping for our clients, we can walk into any store, glance over the racks, pull items, and have at least 15 items in the dressing room in less than 10 minutes. Stores such as Nordstrom Rack, T.J. Maxx, and Marshalls are among our favorite discount stores. The following tips are useful when shopping for discounts or sales:

8. Double check all items for perfection. Look for missing buttons or belts and if you really love it, ask the cashier to give you an additional percentage off. Once you get it home, you can reinvent it with your own style!

9. Shop out of season for items that will not go out of style, like your CORE wardrobe pieces.

10. Check for the quality of sewing. Is the threading about to unravel?

To keep up with the latest trends, go window shopping, look through style magazines, and/or sign up for fashion sites, like **http://www.whowhatwear.com** or for a more mature site, try **http://www.fabulousafter40.com**.

Note to shopaholics: "I can relate. I would spend endless hours shopping and then spend hours returning things. Shopping became a habit and a burning addiction that temporarily filled a void. Finding other ways to occupy your time is much more rewarding. Volunteering, doing something nice for a friend out of the blue, and/or planning an impromptu date with your sweetheart are perfect examples. Nowadays, when I'm not shopping as a profession, I spend my free afternoons volunteering at an animal shelter. (I have a little confession. I just fibbed; I do have a relapse from time to time. It's my job. I have to look stylish!) However, animals never fail to fill my heart with love and gratitude." —*Rayne*

Do yourself the honor of setting a strict shopping budget. Having a clear idea of what you plan on buying will create a win-win situation for you, your closet, and your bank account. They will all remain full and first rate!

Ultimate Guide to Style: From Drab to Fab!

CHAPTER 14

Last Looks: Style Solutions and Tips

This chapter was written to remind you of all the previous tips mentioned throughout the book, along with quick solutions to keep fashion disasters from happening to you. Feel free to print these pages and keep them handy. If you started a style vision board (Chapter 2), you might want to place it there. We just could not resist leaving you with a few more tips to help you LOOK better and FEEL better than you ever thought you could!

Tips to Remember Before You Shop:

* Buy what you like and what fits you, not what you think is in fashion at the time. Just because Lady Gaga is wearing a telephone hat, doesn't mean you have to wear one. If you don't feel 100% comfortable in it, most likely, you will not wear it.

* If you have too many of the same thing, there's no need to buy more. For example, if you already have 10 leopard print silk tops or 5 pairs of black slacks, you have enough.

143

* **Update the items you already have in your closet.** Alter your items to a perfect fit. Change up accessories like scarves and jewelry or replace dull buttons on a sweater with funky cool ones.

Tips for Wardrobe Pairing:
* **Pick one item and let it shine.** If you're wearing an eye catching accessory, such as an animal print scarf, allow it to take the spotlight by pairing it with something simple and understated. For example, an all-white outfit or blue jeans paired with a plain t-shirt and simple shoes can offset a "leopard scarf" purrr-fectly.
* **Avoid wearing all black.** Add a pop of color with accessories. You will draw more positive attention by wearing color.
* **Buckle up...for fashion.** A belt will add a finishing touch to almost any ensemble.
* **Pair something shiny with a matte solid.** To get more use out of your sequined shirts, skirts or pants, pair them with casual and comfortable solid colored t-shirts or jeans.

Before Leaving the House

Before leaving the house, look into a FULL LENGTH mirror to see if you have any of the following problems. Below each problem, we list the solution:

Visible Panty Lines:
Buy seamless underwear or cotton g-strings.

Scuffed Shoes/Bags:
Use a felt tip marker or shoe polish to camouflage scuffs.

Clothing That is Too Tight or Too Short:

Let it go! If you have even the slightest thought that it may be too tight or too revealing, trust yourself, it is.

Check for Missing/Loose Buttons, Snaps, and Hooks:

If you think no one will notice, they will. If you can't repair them yourself, take them to your tailor.

Drooping Hems/Linings:

You guessed it. Take it to a tailor. Avoid taping or stapling hems with your desk stapler!

Lint or Dandruff:

Keep a lint brush with you at home, in your car, and at your office. Scotch tape is also very accessible and it works.

Roots:

Keep yourself on a regular hair maintenance program. Include it in your budget. For visible roots, keep hair up in a bun, ponytail, or try 'hair mascara'. It instantly covers up gray roots. Wear beautiful necklaces/bracelets to draw attention away from your hair.

Chipped Nails:

When getting a manicure, bring in your own nail polish. This way you can paint over any chips later and make the color last longer. You can also ask your nail salon for "gel" nail polish for your finger nails. This will last up to two weeks. It's amazing.

Eyeglass Lenses:

If you prefer to wear glasses instead of contact lenses, make sure the lenses are non-glare.

Spills & Stains on Clothing:

Keep "Wet Ones" or "Tide Sticks" handy. Gently wipe off the spill until you can wash it.

Wrinkled Clothing:

If you're at home, throw the item in the dryer with a damp towel. When you go shopping, look for these synthetic blends: spandex, nylon, acetate, polyester, rayon-blends, and most knits (sweaters with cashmere, wool, etc.). These manmade fabrics rarely wrinkle.

"In-a-pinch shoe insert: Use a thin panty liner to prevent slipping heels and/or sweaty feet. I was at a formal event wearing a new pair of peek-a-boo high heels and they kept slipping off. I had to figure out something or I was going to walk right out of my shoes. I went to the ladies room, looked in my clutch, and had an "ah ha" moment. I quickly inserted the liners into each shoe and no one knew any different."

—*Stacy Ensweiler, friend and entrepreneur*

CHAPTER 15

Last Looks for Men: Style Solutions and Tips

Do you have or know a man who refuses to listen to your advice on wearing white gym socks with black slacks, high waters, UGG boots, or tight pants with his gut spilling over? These are big fashion no-nos. Show him this section NOW!

"One time I wore flip flops with socks on stage and got heckled. Ever since then, I follow my sister's advice on what to wear. No more hecklers!"

—*Erik Hagstrom, singer of The Cocanuts and Rayne's brother*

As two professionals who have been studying men's attire for years, we encourage you manly creatures to consider the suggested guidelines below. Through experience, we know the turn-offs and the turn-ons when it comes to your wardrobe and your image. No, your special girl isn't crazy when she tells you that socks with Birkenstocks aren't attractive and no, we don't like long toe nails, either. Our goal is to help change your shopping "woes" into leisurely "whees"!

We Recommend These Key Essentials:

* A two or three-button suit (choose a color that complements your skin tone).

* A tweed sport coat.

* Six dress shirts in a variety of colors.

* Six plain cotton t-shirts.

* Sharp looking ties.

* Two pocket squares a.k.a. hankies that go into your outer coat pocket.

* Three sweaters, preferably cashmere.

> "I wear long sleeved collared shirts, even when I'm at home. I just feel better when I look nice."
>
> —Nick Militello, friend and movie director

* An overcoat (if you're in a climate that gets chilly).

* Two pairs of jeans: one medium wash for day, one dark colored for evening.

* One pair of cargo, khakis, or carpenter pants.

* Brown belt.

* Black belt.

* Watch.

* Dress shoes.

* Black slip-ons or boots, depending on your preferred style.
* Non-athletic sneaker (Tom's, Converse, and Ryz make some great options).

Even if you don't purchase them all at once, print this list and check it off as you acquire these items. This will help make getting ready a no brainer. You can mix and match according to the season and occasion. Replace a dull button with a bright colored one. Your profession and age will also play key factors. For example, a college man in his 20's may trade a pair of slacks for a pair of jeans. A more expressive gentleman may want to exchange the black slip-ons for blue suede shoes or white leather. You have free reign here. These items will prevent you from looking like a couch potato or nerd.

Colorful striped ties can add vibrancy to your wardrobe, too. Even if you choose to dress more conservatively, you can let your personality shine with a unique tie of your choice. Crazy print shirts can add pizzazz for those of you who like to grab more attention.

We also recommend that you determine your body type and buy these key essentials accordingly.

You should look good and feel good in your own wardrobe. Remember to stay true to your personality. Every man deserves to "strut his stuff."

What to Wear on a Date

If you're single and dating, keep in mind that you only get one shot at making a first impression. If you're in a relationship or married, avoid letting your appearance slip. Show your personality when you dress.

We have both been on blind dates where no matter how great the man was we just couldn't get past his unappealing wardrobe. If your wardrobe is sloppy or out-of-date, we can only imagine what your house looks like. We assume it's messy, dirty, and disheveled. Don't judge us, we can't help it! Matchmaking agencies love to use our makeover services, since we are the "go to gals" for turning their clients from drab to fab. Their goal is to have you looking and feeling your best, as you will have a better shot at finding love under those terms.

When choosing an outfit for a date, think twice before you throw on an all-black suit, since it can come off as generic, uninviting, and/or looking as if you have something to prove. We want to see you get a second and third date. Focus on a more casual look that gives off a down to earth, friendly, and confident vibe. We suggest a soft cashmere sweater or soft button up shirt, dark colored jeans, black socks, and snazzy shoes. If the date is a little more formal, add a cool blazer or non-black suit with a colorful tie. You can always refer to this quick checklist for a refresher.

Formal Date

Tops:
* Blazer/sport coat with a crisp button up shirt.

Bottoms:
* Slacks.

Shoes:
* Loafers or lace-ups.
* Snazzy shoes.

Casual Date

Tops:

* Light-weight cotton t-shirts or polos in complementing colors.
* Casual jacket or cashmere sweater, just in case it gets cold.

Bottoms:

* Dark jeans for evening and medium wash for daytime.
* Loafers/slip-ons.
* Straight or relaxed cut pants.
* Non-athletic sneakers.
* Boots.

Things Women Will Notice and Find Sexy!

1. Classy watch that makes a subtle statement.
2. Colorful shirts. Wearing black ages almost everyone, makes you look tired, and comes off cold.
3. Well-fitting clothing (not too baggy or too tight).
4. Fantastic and clean shoes; they tell a lot about a person.
5. Stand proud and smile! Great posture can make you look better in your clothes, 10 pounds lighter, and 100 times more confident. Along with these, a beautiful smile can break the ice, warm hearts, and brighten up someone's day.

What to Wear to an Interview

How can you make yourself stand out in the interviewer's mind after he or she sees six other possible candidates for the job? Instead of wearing a suit in black, go for a navy blue or gray suit with a colorful button-up shirt. We prefer a blue or teal shirt with a nice classy silk tie, yet a white shirt works if you're on the more conservative side. For shoes, we recommend a dark colored lace-up, preferably black.

Grooming Tips

Manscaping: Trim your body hair...please. If you have back hair, you can wax it, shave it, or have it professionally lasered. If you have long chest, arm, and/or unruly hair "down there," you can buy some clippers to get a nice trim. We recommend Cruzer by Braun available online at http://www.braun.com. Braun also has ear and nose hair trimmers. Trust us, this is a necessity.

Maintain nice hands and nails. If you don't take care of them, we question what else you don't take care of.

Keep up a nice smile. If you have lost some of your teeth, please get them replaced. Ask your dentist about veneers. Veneers are Hollywood's best kept secret for amazing teeth. As with the ladies, you can help keep your teeth bright and white with professional bleaching at your dentist's office or at home with Crest White Strips.

Before Leaving the House

Before leaving the house, look in a FULL LENGTH mirror to see if you have any of the following:

We suggest that you shop with a friend who you know will give you an honest opinion or hire us to help you. Wink-wink!

After reading these tips, we hope that you found them useful for the next time you shop. Along with your fabulous wardrobe, remember to be chivalrous. A man who is polite, opens doors, and smiles can charm the pants off of anyone. Look at George Clooney!

Problem	Solution
Scuffed shoes	Use a felt tip marker or shoe polish to cover them.
Tight pants	Try a "relax fit waistband". Your waist size can fluctuate up to four inches.
Faded clothing	If you have even the slightest thought that it may be too tight or too faded; trust yourself, it is. Even though you love it, let it go.
Missing or loose buttons/snaps	If you think no one will notice, they will. Either repair them yourself, or take them to your tailor.
Skin showing over the socks	Wear over-the-calf socks (not with shorts).
Flimsy collar	Use collar stays in plastic or metal to keep them looking crisp.
Collar too tight	Use a collar extender which lets you add half a size to your shirt so dressing up becomes a much more comfortable experience.
Shirt tail bunched	Tuck it into your underwear.
Out of control tie	Use a tie clip.
Balding	Shave your head. No comb overs. It's more work but so worth it. We love rubbing a man's bald head.
Lint or dandruff	Keep a lint brush with you at home, in your car, and at the office.
Glasses drift down on nose	Have glasses refitted.
Eyeglass lenses	Contacts are recommended. We want to see your eyes. If you must wear glasses, make sure they are a flattering shape for your face and the lenses are non-glare.
Green eyeglass nose pieces	Buy titanium frames or wash them every day with soapy water.
Spills & stains on clothing	Keep "Wet Ones" or "Tide Sticks" handy.
Wrinkled clothes	Buy non-iron shirts or a steamer. This is way easier than ironing. You can also hang the shirt in the bathroom with you as you shower. The steam will help take out the wrinkles.

Note: We used the term "charm the pants off" for an effect. We wouldn't recommend that you actually charm the pants off your boss or your girlfriend's sister. This could definitely get you into trouble!

Ultimate Guide to Style: From Drab to Fab!

Afterword

*U*ltimate Guide to Style was written to be self-empowering, confidence boosting, and eye-opening. Maybe like us, you're not a perfect ten, yet we hope that this book has given you a greater appreciation for the FABULOUS reflection staring back at you. We want nothing more than for you to walk away using this guide's information as a tool so you can LOOK better and FEEL better than you ever thought you could. We did warn you that we would be saying that a lot!

We are so pleased that you have taken the time to learn about the best possible fashion choices for yourself, just as we took the time to learn how to write this book. We laughed, we threw tantrums, and one of us (we will not say who) even cried. Okay, we admit it, we both did. This adventure continues to challenge us to be stronger women, not only for ourselves, but also for our family, clients, friends, and now you… our readers. After all, life is all about the journey and the beautiful souls we meet along the way.

We lovingly thank you from the bottom of our shopping bags for all of your support!

Fashionably Yours,

Rayne Parvis and Nicole Drake
http://www.StyleByRayne.com
http://www.NicoleDrake.com

Acknowledgements

If we win a Pulitzer Prize here is what you will hear as part of our long drawn out "slightly intoxicated" celebratory speech. We recommend getting comfortable:

Tom Antion, without your patience, dedication to our success, and guidance, this book would not exist. You are the best business mentor EVER!

Our clients, whose comments are spread throughout this book, thank you for letting us be a part of your beautiful transformations.

Karen A. Bayer at *Meet the Perfect You*, thank you for believing in us and sending us so many lovely clients. We feel so blessed.

A very special thank you to the following for their tremendous Kickstarter contribution of $100 or more to getting this book made: Tom Antion, Dov Baron, Jennifer Beinash, Mary Cimiluca, Beth Drake Ryzyk, Joanie Fare, Daniel Hall, Jenn Levy, Ursula Mentjes, Audessa Siccardi, Sean Stevens, and Dusty White. There are so many more friends through Kickstarter that contributed and supported us in getting this book made. We greatly appreciate all of you.

To our fantastic sketch artist, Sharon Hagstrom, thank you for your outstanding creativity and talent. Betsy Pettet, your graphics are impeccable and add such nice touch.

Anita Bullard, Joanie Fare, and Sharon Hagstrom, we appreciate all your assistance in proofreading our book.

Audessa Siccardi, thank you for your contribution to the color chapter. We love it!

Rachel Lorber, thank you for implementing dozens of nitpicking notes, and many hours of Photoshop.

Matthew T. Collins, thank you for always take such fabulous photos of us.

To Our Family, Thank You for
Your Love and Neverending Support:

From Nicole: Thank you to Chloe Drake, Edward Bahia, Frank Drake, Mary Jo Klingbeil, and Rayne Parvis.

From Rayne: My family: My beloved dad, "**Wayne** the Stain", thank you for encouraging me to pursue my dreams, to stand-up for what I believe in, and to never give up. Your belief in me as an individual and creator has given me such amazing ground to stand on. **Erik** Hagstrom, my sweet brother, I am sorry for trying to poison you with berries as a young child. The Versaces, my support for your amazing band; **http://www.TheCocanuts.com** your dirty dishes I clean up, and the beer money I give you, are only small actions to show you how grateful I am for you. Your heart, love, and ability to forgive, inspires me to be a better human. **Sharon** Hagstrom, my favorite mom, you have worked your butt off in so many ways to support our family's creative pursuits of happiness. Without you, we would have no instruments to play, no music to record, no performances to practice for, and no books to write. You are the glue that holds the family together. My sister, **Lia** Franz, you are miles away, and in my heart you will always stay. **Sylvia** and **Star,** my four-legged furry family, your understanding of the human emotion is remarkable. Your unforgettable souls will always remain in the "happy thought" section of my brain. **Distant Relatives** in the distance, thank you! **My friends:** Carla Shammas, Candace Rocha, Jenn Levy, Nick Militello, Jill Brazelton, Christian Dorris, Marlena Bansberg, Rachel Lorber, Rosalyn and Rozan Mardosian, Karen Lesetmoe, Karla Weller, your never ending friendship and sacrificing support through the years leaves me speechless (for once). Thank you for loving me exactly the way I am...nowhere near perfect. Sammy Oriti, I have grown so much from all that you taught me; from saving turtles to sh*tting in a bucket (joke) to planting the seed of Jesus, I am a better women because I knew you. Harmony Dust, my Type A partner, thank you for your constant prayers and words of wisdom. Amy Redman, thank you for helping me leave the nest. Thank you, **http://www. abclyde.com,** your comedic music puts a smile on my face. **My parent's friends:** thank you for all your support and fabulous holiday dinners over the years. **Tom Antion,** I know we already thanked you. However, I have a little more to thank you for; teaching me how to be a business women, for holding my hand through times I didn't believe in myself, for not being satisfied with anything less than my best, for sitting me down in that airport and demanding I start this book, for being so inspirational and honest in your ethics, for being so kind… for being you. I thank God for you every day. And last but not least, **Nicole Drake:** Thank you for being a part of this journey. It wouldn't be as sweet without you. Your kind heart and soft approach is a trait that is admirable. I love you and I am so proud of you.

Holy crapola! I almost forgot the **Holy Trinity.** I am in amazement by your clever guidance, impact, and constant gentle pursuit of my heart. I know I can be stubborn. Thank you for never leaving me or forsaking me.

Note from Rayne: Sorry I had such a long thank you section. I am aware that I didn't win an Oscar, or a Pulitzer Prize or cure world hunger, however, it's my first book, so I may have got a little carried away. THANK YOU AGAIN!

Fashion Glossary

A-Line Dress	"A" shaped dress that skims the wearer's form and flares out to a full skirt from the waist.
Bandeau	A woman's strapless top formed from a band of fabric fitting around the bust.
Blazer	A type of suit-like jacket.
Bodice	The top part of a woman's dress (excluding sleeves) that is above the waist.
Bohemian	Fashion trend associated with a free-spirited, poetic, romantic, or folkloric attitude feel.
Boot-Cut	Fitted pants that flare slightly out from the knees to allow for boots or other footwear.
Boy-Leg	Shorts or underwear that have tight-fitting legs to the top of the thigh.
Brocade	A fabric woven with a raised pattern.
Cameltoe	A slang term that refers to the outline of a woman's "lady parts" seen through tight pants at the crotch area.
Camisole/Cami	Spaghetti strapped tank top, usually worn under a light weight sweater.
Capri Pants	Fitted pants that extend down to mid-calf level.
Charmeuse	A glistening smooth, drapery fabric often in silk.

Cropped Pants	Pants that end right above the ankles.
Cropped Top/Jacket	Top or jacket that ends near and above the waist.
Cowl Neck	Usually a sweater, with a high loose-fitting turnover collar.
Dark Wash	Dark blue jeans that have been prewashed.
Dart	A stitched trick to make the garment fit better.
Double-Breasted	One side of the garment overlaps the edge of another, with two rows of buttons/fasteners.
Drape	A garment's hang or fall
Embellishments	Extra adornments added to a piece of clothing such as beads, pearls, sequins, buttons, embroidery, etc.
Empire	Garment with seam just under the bust, rather than waist, creating a flattering sweep.
Faux Leather	Synthetic material that looks like leather, but is man-made and animal free.
Flare Pants	Pants that fit straight through hip and flare out at the bottom.
Flat-Front Pants	Fitted pants without tucks, pleats, or pockets in the front.
Form-Fitting/ Slim-Fit	Style in which the fabric is fitted directly from the waist to the ankle (with a curve for the hip).

Halter Top	Bodice without sleeves that is supported by a strap or fabric that wraps around the neck and often without a back.
High-Low Hem	Hemline that is not even, falls from the front to the back or from one side to the other, with a higher hemline in front.
Hip-Huggers	Pants starting at and hugging the hips below the natural waist to make the torso appear longer.
Leather	Tanned or hide of a cow or other animal.
Maxi Dress	A floor or ankle length informal dress, formfitting at the top and loose flowing at the bottom, cut to flow over the body. They come in a variety of necklines, colors and patterns.
Merino	Cotton like wool, resembling cashmere.
Minimizer	A bra that minimizes the appearance of your bust by 1-2 inches.
Moisture-Wickin	Materials created to draw perspiration from the outer skin.
Monochromatic	Various hues of one color.
Monokini	Two-piece bathing suits with top and bottoms connected by string, chain, or fabric on the front.
Nylon/ Lycra Spandex	A fabric blend with nylon-like strength and spandex elasticity.
Off-The-Shoulder	Neckline sitting lightly over the top of the bust-line and off the shoulders.

Pilling	The normal wear and tear of manmade fabrics that cause "little balls of fabric" to appear on the outer layer of clothing.
Polyester	Man-made fabric with a ultitude of finishes.
Rayon	Man-made silky material easily draped and dyed.
Rhinestones	An imitation diamond.
Ruching	Gathered, textured or ruffled effect created with pleating or shirring.
Ruffle	Rippled lace or ribbon at an edge.
Satin	Shiny, smooth fabric.
Scoop/ Round Neck	Low neckline that is round or "U" shaped.
Shapewear	Undergarments designed to mold or hold a body to a certain shape, like a girdle.
Sheath Dress	Close fitting, straight style dress.
Shirring	Gathering up of material.
Silk	Exceptionally soft material made naturally by silkworms.
Spaghetti Strap	Thin shoulder-strap connected to the bodice.
Spandex	Stretchy shiny fabric.
Straight Legs	Legs that go straight down without thinning or widening from the top to the bottom.
Straight Skirt	Straight and plain skirt. Hem and waistline have no flare or fullness.

Structured Jackets	Shaped and fit to the body with buttons, curved seams, and darts.
Suede	Textured leather, slightly raised on the inside to create a nap.
Taffeta	A fine lustrous silk or similar synthetic fabric with a crisp texture.
Tank	Top with thin straps, a rounded neck, and deep holes for arms.
Tankini	Two-piece swimsuit with the top being a tank top style.
Powernet	A tummy control lining often used in bathing suits.
Tube Top	A tight-fitting strapless top made of stretchy material.
Tunic	Slip-on garment that falls at or below the hips.
Turtleneck	High, tight neck on a top.
Tweed	Rough material used for coats or other semi-casual garments.
V-Neck	The neck of a garment has the shape in front of the letter V.
Whiskering	The fading or pulling of <u>creases</u> in <u>blue jeans</u>, especially around the <u>crotch</u>.
Wide Leg	Referring to pants that are wide from waist to bottom with no flare or hugging of the leg.

Ultimate Guide to Style: From Drab to Fab!

References and Resources

Stores and clothing lines mentioned in this book:

Adidas

Aerin Rose

Baekgaard

Body Language Sportswear

Chanel

Cole Haan

Converse

Dior

eBay

Forever 21

Frederick's of Hollywood (VaVa Voom)

Giorgio Armani

Goodwill

Gucci

H&M

Hello Kitty

Hermes Birkin

JCPenney

Krisa

Louis Vuitton

Lulu Lemon

Macy's

Marshalls

MilkStars

Nation (LTD Oregon Tee)

Naturalizer

New Balance

Neiman Marcus

Nike

Nordstrom Rack

Pink

Poshmark

Prada

Ray-Ban

Ross

Ryz

Salvation Army

Sofft Shoe

Sold Design Lab

Spanx   Tom's
Stella McCartney   UGGS
Sunsets Inc.   Versace
Swim Systems   Victoria's Secret
T.J. Maxx   Wacoal
Target   Walmart

Websites

For what's hot now:
www.Whowhatwear.com

www.Refinery29.com

For what's hot now, women over 40:
www.Fabulousafterforty.com

Where to sell your items online:
www.Poshmark.com

www.eBay.com

Where to get your 3 ounces or less for travel?
www.3floz.com

Books References

Veronique Henderson (Author) and Pat Henshaw (Author) *Color Me Beautiful, Color Me Younger*

Clinton Kelly (Author), Stacy London (Author) *Dress Your Best: The Complete Guide to Finding the Style That's Right for Your Body*

Victoria Moran (Author), *Creating a Charmed Life*

Image Credits

Christine P. Flores on **www.fiverr.com** username Sweet Christine, cartoonist: Rayne and Nicole front cover images, all body-shapes: Pear, Apple, Rectangle, Hourglass, Extra-curvy, Sadie (pitbull before and after), Baby Chloe with necklace, and Erik Hagstrom

Sharon Hagstrom, original sketch artist: all clothing sketches, maxi-dress, bathing suits, scarfs (1-4), face shapes

Betsy Pettet, graphic artist who turned Sharon's body shape wardrobe sketches into a computerized form, colored them, and made them pop: all clothing sketches

Shutterstock: pink armoire, three working girl cartoons, five girls with pink flowers

Matthew T. Collins, photographer: Rayne and Nicole (About Author page)

Samar Hazboun, photographer: Rayne (About Author page)

Get your
Free Style and Fashion Consultation
with Audessa Siccardi
- Best Selling Author with Dr. Wayne Dyer
Style to Make You Look Younger
Colors to Attract Love, Success & Money
Fashion to Allure Your Soul Mate
Audessa Siccardi
"Stylist in Alluring Fashion & Image"
Audessa@AudessaInc.com
Make Your Life Easier & Call Now: 760-415-5510
WWW. AUDESSAINC.COM
We give 10% of all retail sales to charity to help others.
Ad by: paolosanchez.com

Frustrated because your business isn't growing?

Learn how to Sell with Intention for FREE for 30 days!

We'll teach you how to:

- **Easily ask for and get the appointment .**

- **Create simple sales scripts .**

- **Close the sale without feeling "bad" .**

- **Follow up quickly .**

- **Double and triple your sales!**

*Cancel at Anytime

www.mysalescoachnow.com

Testimonial:

I find great value in being a member of the Sales Coach Now community! I eagerly await my CD each month. I can truly say that I have implemented many ideas and connected with a number of experts that you've featured on Conversation and Coffee.

Robin Allen - Certified Nutrition Specialist

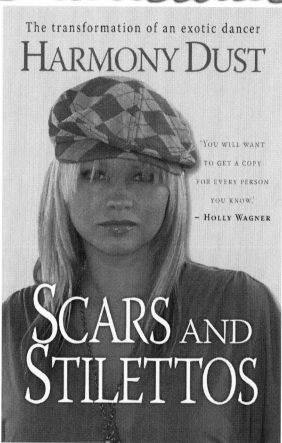

BetsyPettet | graphic design and illustration

www.betsypettet.com
(818) 599 0700

illustration
vector artwork
website design
photography
graphic design
packaging

Are you ready
for your future?

Our doors are open.

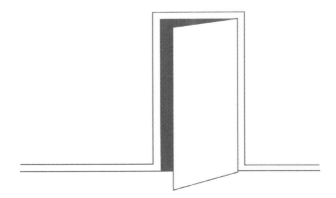

Build Profitable Websites
Create & Sell Your Own Products
Manage Website Sales & Marketing

Contact us to talk about
your future on the Internet.

1-757-687-5190

For detailed information about
Internet marketing visit us as

www.imtcva.org

*Internet**Marketing***
TRAINING CENTER

State Council of
Higher Education for Virginia